# PRAXIS® 5169 Middle School Mathematics

## The PRAXIS® Series

## By: Preparing Teachers In America™

This page is intentionally left blank.

This page is intentionally left blank.

**Free Online Email Tutoring Services**

All preparation guides purchased directly from Preparing Teachers In America includes a free three month email tutoring subscription. Any resale of preparation guides does not qualify for a free email tutoring subscription.

## What is Email Tutoring?

Email Tutoring allows buyers to send questions to tutors via email. Buyers can send any questions regarding the exam processes, strategies, content questions, or practice questions.

Preparing Teachers In America reserves the right not to answer questions with or without reason(s).

## How to use Email Tutoring?

Buyers need to send an email to onlinepreparationservices@gmail.com requesting email tutoring services. Buyers may be required to confirm the email address used to purchase the preparation guide or additional information prior to using email tutoring. Once email tutoring subscription is confirmed, buyers will be provided an email address to send questions to. The three month period will start the day the subscription is confirmed.

Any misuse of email tutoring services will result in termination of service. Preparing Teachers In America reserves the right to terminate email tutoring subscription at anytime with or without notice.

**Comments and Suggestions**

All comments and suggestions for improvements for the study guide and email tutoring services need to be sent to onlinepreparationservices@gmail.com.

This page is intentionally left blank.

# Table of Content

About the Exam and Study Guide..................................................................................1

Exam Answer Sheet – Test 1.......................................................................................5

Middle School Practice Exam Questions – Test 1.........................................................7

Middle School Practice Exam Answers – Test 1..........................................................37

Middle School Practice Exam Questions and Explanations – Test 1............................39

Exam Answer Sheet – Test 2.....................................................................................99

Middle School Practice Exam Questions – Test 2.....................................................101

Middle School Practice Exam Answers – Test 2........................................................131

Middle School Practice Exam Questions and Explanations – Test 2..........................133

Exam Answer Sheet – Test 3....................................................................................195

Middle School Practice Exam Questions – Test 3.....................................................197

Middle School Practice Exam Answers – Test 3........................................................227

Middle School Practice Exam Questions and Explanations – Test 3..........................229

This page is intentionally left blank.

## About the Exam and Study Guide

**What is the PRAXIS Middle Grades Mathematics Exam?**

The PRAXIS Middle Grades Mathematics is an exam to measure potential teachers' competencies in mathematics knowledge related to middle school grade levels. The test measures whether individuals have the knowledge necessary to start teaching middle school math. The exam is based largely on teacher preparation standards, and the following are content areas covered by the middle school math exam:

- Number Sense and Operations
- Algebra and Functions
- Measurement and Geometry
- Statistics and Probability

The exam is timed at 2 hours and consists of 55 questions. The 55 selected-response questions or numerical-entry questions are based on knowledge obtained in a bachelor's degree program. The exam contains some questions that may not count toward the score. Calculators are permitted on the exam.

**What topics are covered on the exam?**

The following are some topics covered on the exam:

- numbers
- operations
- patterns, relations, and functions
- algebraic techniques and applications
- nonlinear relations and concepts of calculus
- measurement principles, procedures, and applications
- geometry in two and three dimensions
- coordinate and transformational geometry
- principles and techniques of statistics
- principles of probability and techniques for determining probability

**What is included in this study guide book?**

This guide includes three full length practice exams for the PRAXIS Middle Grades Mathematics along with detail explanations. The recommendation is to take the tests under timed exam conditions and a quiet environment.

This page is intentionally left blank.

# Practice Test 1

This page is intentionally left blank.

# Exam Answer Sheet – Test 1

Below is an optional answer sheet to use to document answers.

| Question Number | Selected Answer | Question Number | Selected Answer |
|---|---|---|---|
| 1 | | 31 | |
| 2 | | 32 | |
| 3 | | 33 | |
| 4 | | 34 | |
| 5 | | 35 | |
| 6 | | 36 | |
| 7 | | 37 | |
| 8 | | 38 | |
| 9 | | 39 | |
| 10 | | 40 | |
| 11 | | 41 | |
| 12 | | 42 | |
| 13 | | 43 | |
| 14 | | 44 | |
| 15 | | 45 | |
| 16 | | 46 | |
| 17 | | 47 | |
| 18 | | 48 | |
| 19 | | 49 | |
| 20 | | 50 | |
| 21 | | 51 | |
| 22 | | 52 | |
| 23 | | 53 | |
| 24 | | 54 | |
| 25 | | 55 | |
| 26 | | | |
| 27 | | | |
| 28 | | | |
| 29 | | | |
| 30 | | | |

This page is intentionally left blank.

**QUESTION 1**

At a high school, the ratio of basketball players to baseball players is 7 to 3, and the ratio of football players to soccer players is 8 to 5. If the ratio of baseball players to soccer players is 1 to 4, then what is the ratio of the basketball players to football players?

    A. $\frac{35}{96}$

    B. $\frac{7}{8}$

    C. $\frac{7}{24}$

    D. $\frac{18}{35}$

**Answer:**

**QUESTION 2**

If the value in the thousands place of the first number is multiplied with the value in the hundreds place in the second number, and this product is added to the value in the thousandths place of the third number, then what number will result from these operations?

    Number 1: 124,587

    Number 2: 25,478.2445

    Number 3: 145.25402

  A. 39

  B. 35

  C. 20

  D. 16

**Answer:**

7

## QUESTION 3

Fifteen people are waiting for the winning numbers for the daily lottery. The age and gender of the 15 people are given below. If there will be a winner among the fifteen people, what is the probability that the winner will be a female or an individual younger than 25?

| Gender | M | F | F | M | M | M | F | F | M | M | F | M | F | F | M |
|--------|---|---|---|---|---|---|---|---|---|---|---|---|---|---|---|
| Age | 24 | 26 | 18 | 18 | 26 | 22 | 24 | 21 | 19 | 25 | 26 | 24 | 32 | 35 | 41 |

**Answer:**

## QUESTION 4

If the value of t, in the equation below, is increased by 2, how will the value of g change?

$$g = 4 \times (t + 2)^2 + 3 \times (t+p) - 5$$

A. 25

B. 16t + 54

C. 16t + 4p + 54

D. 54

**Answer:**

8

## QUESTION 5

The position of a particle moving in an accelerator is given by $p(t) = 2t^3 - 4t^2 + 2t - 1$. What is the position of the particle at $t = 4$ seconds?

    A.  23

    B.  43

    C.  71

    D.  7943

**Answer:**

## QUESTION 6

Two trapezoids are shown in the figure below. Trapezoid 1 has height of 8 in, a base of 10 in, and an area of 148 in$^2$. Trapezoid 2 has height of 16 in and a base of 20 in. If the two trapezoids are similar, what is the length of the other base in Trapezoid 2?

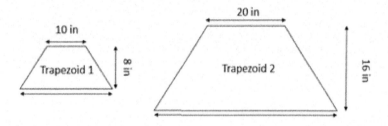

    A.  12 in

    B.  27 in

    C.  54 in

    D.  Not enough information

**Answer:**

# QUESTION 7

In the figure below, angle A is equal to x – 24 degrees. If angle B is equal to x – 36 degrees, then what is the value of x?

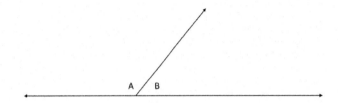

    A. 84°

    B. 86°

    C. 120°

    D. 180°

**Answer:**

# QUESTION 8

A university counselor was asked to report on the number of students enrolled in the five different colleges at the university. The counselor was asked to also report on the number of males and females in each of those five colleges. The data the counselor obtained is shown below. Which of the following graphs accurately represent the data obtained?

|  | Males | Females | Total |
|---|---|---|---|
| **College of Business** | 250 | 300 | 550 |
| **College of Engineering** | 162 | 85 | 247 |
| **College of Liberal Arts** | 144 | 225 | 369 |
| **College of Natural Sciences** | 325 | 336 | 661 |
| **College of Technology** | 114 | 96 | 210 |

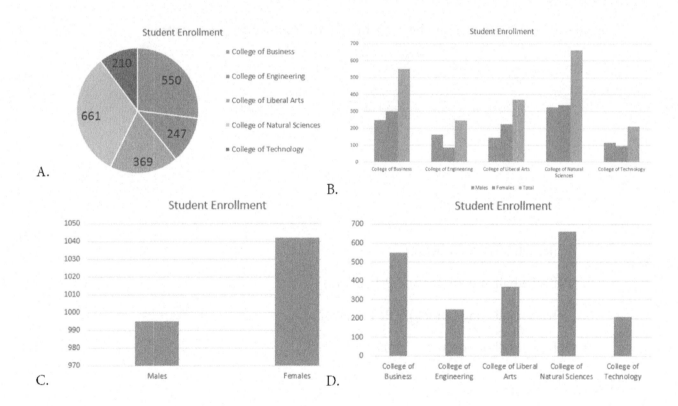

A.

B.

C.

D.

**Answer:**

## QUESTION 9

One letter will be randomly selected from the set below. What is the probability that is a vowel or precedes the letter G in alphabetical order?

$$\{A, B, C, L, M, N, O, P, E, F, H, I, T, S, V, U\}$$

    A. 0.0977

    B. 0.3125

    C. 0.5000

    D. 0.6250

**Answer:**

## QUESTION 10

Considering the Venn diagram below, which of the following options is true?

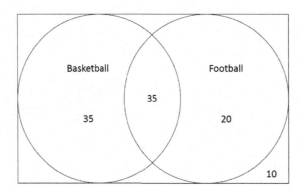

    A. P(Basketball) < P(Football)

    B. P(Basketball and Football) < P(Football)

    C. P(Basketball and Football) > P(Basketball)

    D. P(Basketball or Football) = 1.00

**Answer:**

**QUESTION 11**

Jacob received the following scores on his first five exams. If there is one more exam Jacob needs to take, then what grade must he receive on that exam to have an overall average of 80?

72, 68, 91, 54, 95

**Answer:**

**QUESTION 12**

Ronald, George and James have each ordered a pizza. Ronald's pizza is 30% larger than George's pizza. James' pizza is 30% larger than George's pizza. Ronald has eaten 37.5% of his pizza. George has about 0.05 of his pizza remaining. James has eaten $\frac{3}{7}$ of his pizza. Approximately, which of the following correctly orders who has eaten the most pizza?

A.  Ronald > James > George

B.  George > James > Ronald

C.  James > George> Ronald

D.  Ronald > George > James

**Answer:**

**QUESTION 13**

Set S contains the following numbers. Which of the following options lists the rational numbers of the set in order from least to greatest?

$$S = \{-1.25 \times 10^{-4}, 5.2 \times 10^3, 0.111, 1.75, \sqrt{2}, \sqrt{-25}, \sqrt{4}, \sqrt{25}, 1.25 \times 10^{-5}, 125478, 145\sqrt{2}, \sqrt{5.2 \times 10^3}\}$$

A. $\{\sqrt{-25}, -1.25 \times 10^{-4}, 1.25 \times 10^{-5}, 0.111, 1.75, \sqrt{4}, \sqrt{25}, \sqrt{5.2 \times 10^3}, 5.2 \times 10^3, 125478\}$

B. $\{-1.25 \times 10^{-4}, 1.25 \times 10^{-5}, 0.111, 1.75, \sqrt{2}, \sqrt{4}, \sqrt{25}, \sqrt{5.2 \times 10^3}, 5.2 \times 10^3, 125478\}$

C. $\{-1.25 \times 10^{-4}, 1.25 \times 10^{-5}, 0.111, 1.75, \sqrt{4}, \sqrt{25}, \sqrt{5.2 \times 10^3}, 5.2 \times 10^3, 125478\}$

D. $\{1.25 \times 10^{-5}, -1.25 \times 10^{-4}, 0.111, 1.75, \sqrt{4}, \sqrt{25}, \sqrt{5.2 \times 10^3}, 5.2 \times 10^3, 125478\}$

**Answer:**

**QUESTION 14**

A bucket consists of red and blue marbles. The red marbles weigh 2 grams and the blue marble weigh 7 grams. The total weight of the bucket is 85 grams. If it is known that there are 2 more red marbles than blue marbles, then what is the total number of marbles in the bucket?

A. 8

B. 9

C. 18

D. 20

**Answer:**

## QUESTION 15

At time 0, Chris leaves work and heads home. The following graphs shows the distance Chris is from work as time goes by. During the period between 1 and 5 minutes, which of the following best describes what Chris was doing?

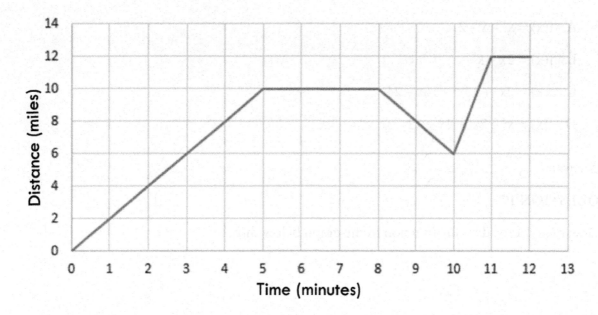

A. Chris is stuck in traffic and is not moving.

B. Chris is heading in a direction towards his workplace.

C. Chris is heading home at a constant speed.

D. Chris has parked his car in his driveway.

**Answer:**

## QUESTION 16

Which of the given equations has the following three zeros and passes through the x values below?

$$x = -1, x = 2, \text{ and } x = -6$$

A. $f(x) = x^2 - x - 2$

B. $f(x) = 2x - x^2$

C. $f(x) = 2x^3 + 10x^2 - 16x - 24$

D. $f(x) = x^3 - 7x^2 + 4x + 12$

**Answer:**

## QUESTION 17

How many zeros does the function in the graph below show?

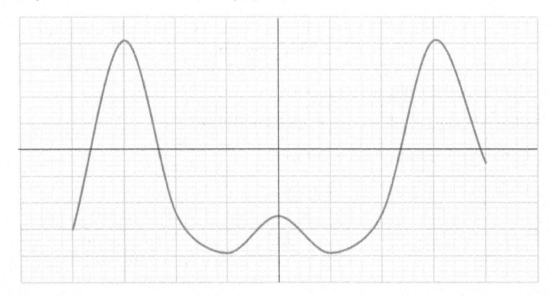

A. 1

B. 2

C. 3

D. 4

**Answer:**

## QUESTION 18

Select the answer choice that does NOT equal to the following rational expression:

$$\frac{m^2 + 9m + 18}{m^2 - m - 12}$$

A. $\frac{(m + 3) \times (m + 6)}{(m - 4) \times (m + 3)}$

B. $\frac{(m + 6)}{(m - 4)}$

C. $\frac{m^2 + 18 + 9m}{m^2 - 12 - m}$

D. $\left(\frac{m^2 + 9m + 18}{m^2 - m - 12}\right)^{-1}$

**Answer:**

**QUESTION 19**

Which of the following options is false?

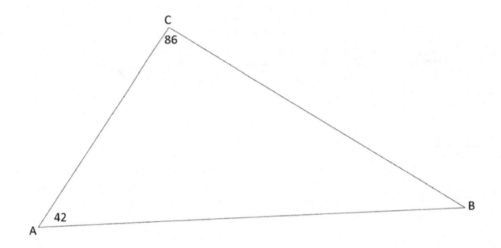

    A. ∡CAB <∡CBA <∡BCA

    B. $\overline{BC}$< $\overline{CA}$<$\overline{BA}$

    C. ∡CAB + ∡CBA + ∡BCA = 180

    D. $\overline{BA}$>$\overline{BC}$>$\overline{CA}$

**Answer:**

**QUESTION 20**

A chair manufacturer can build a maximum of 200 chairs in one month. The manufacturer takes orders of 5 chairs per order. For the month of March, the manufacturer has already secured orders for a total of 120 chairs. What is the maximum number of orders the manufacturer can add to the production for March?

    A. 16

    B. 40

    C. 80

    D. 120

**Answer:**

## QUESTION 21

Which number line below graphically represents the answer to the following inequality?

$$|4x + 12| < 2x + 12$$

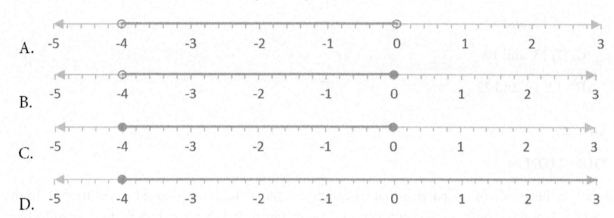

A.

B.

C.

D.

**Answer:**

## QUESTION 22

Which of the following options is a median for the isosceles triangle shown below?

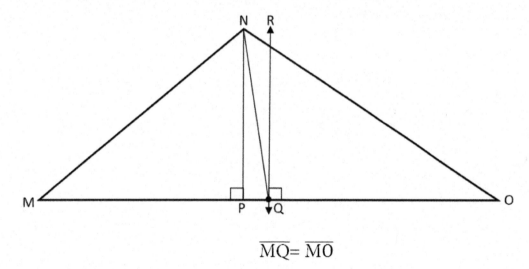

$$\overline{MQ} = \overline{MO}$$

A. $\overline{NP}$

B. $\overleftrightarrow{RQ}$

C. $\overline{NQ}$

D. $\overline{MQ}$

**Answer:**

**QUESTION 23**

Which of the following sets of numbers cannot be the measurements of the sides of a triangle?

    A. 6, 8, and 10

    B. 9, 12, and 22

    C. 7, 13, and 19

    D. 12, 19, and 25

**Answer:**

**QUESTION 24**

John has been told by his parents that he can no longer spend more than $100 per month. In the first week of the month, John spent $14 on a movie ticket. In the second week, John spend $12 at the arcade. In the third week, John chose not to spend any money, so he could spend more the following week at his friend's birthday party. Which of the following number lines most accurately shows how much money John can spend in the last week of the month?

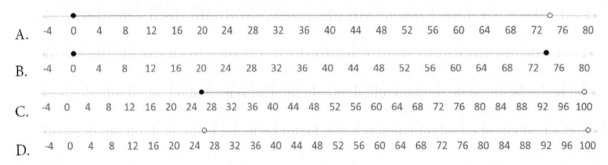

**Answer:**

## QUESTION 25

A mechanic charges $50 an hour to fix a car and requires 65% reimbursement of any additional costs needed to fix the car. If the mechanic had to purchase $350 worth of the equipment to fix the car, how much of this cost will be paid back to the mechanic.

    A. $122.50

    B. $227.50

    C. $277.50

    D. $350.00

**Answer:**

## QUESTION 26

If a < b < - 1 < 0 < 1 < c < d, then which of the following fractions has the smallest value?

    A. $\dfrac{b}{a}$

    B. $\dfrac{c}{d}$

    C. $\dfrac{0}{c}$

    D. $\dfrac{d}{b}$

**Answer:**

## QUESTION 27

What digit will be in the hundreds place of $1.25468 \times 10^{25}$?

    A. 0

    B. 6

    C. 5

    D. 2

**Answer:**

**QUESTION 28**

In parallelogram MNOP, ∢M = x + 15 and ∢N = 3x + 5. What is the value of ∢P?

**Answer:**

**QUESTION 29**

What is the result of performing this multiplication?

$$(-15 + 3i) \times (5 + 4i)$$

A.  -87 – 45i

B.  -87 – 33i

C.  -63 – 45i

D.  -63 – 33i

**Answer:**

**QUESTION 30**

What value(s) of x will satisfy the following equation?

$$18x^2 + 24x + 8 = 0$$

A.  0

B.  -2/3

C.  2/3

D.  2/3 and -2/3

**Answer:**

## QUESTION 31

John's weekly income consists of his hourly wages and a $50 weekly allowance given to him by his father. Maria's weekly income consists of her hourly wages and a weekly allowance given to her by her father. John earns $10 an hour and Maria earns $12 an hour. If they each work for 10 hours in one week, how much weekly allowance does Maria's father need to give her, so both Maria and John earn the same income in that week?

    A.  $20

    B.  $30

    C.  $50

    D.  $120

**Answer:**

## QUESTION 32

Solve for x and y:

$$12x + 12y = 40$$
$$8x + 4y = 32$$

    A.  $x = -11\frac{1}{3}$ and $y = 14\frac{2}{3}$

    B.  $x = -1\frac{5}{9}$ and $y = 4\frac{8}{9}$

    C.  $x = 4\frac{2}{3}$ and $y = -8\frac{1}{3}$

    D.  $x = 4\frac{2}{3}$ and $y = -1\frac{1}{3}$

**Answer:**

## QUESTION 33

The graph below represents the solution to which of the following inequalities

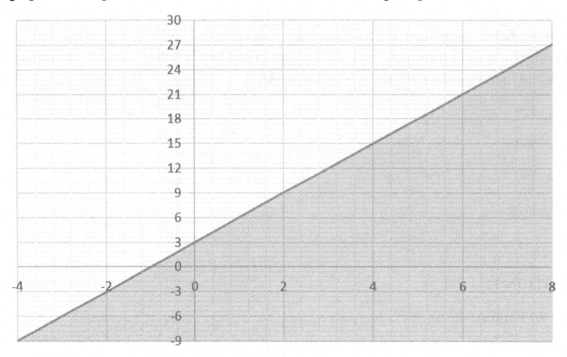

A. $y < -3x - 3$

B. $y \leq 3x + 3$

C. $y < 3x + 3$

D. $y \geq 3x + 3$

**Answer:**

**QUESTION 34**

What are the next three numbers in the following sequence?

$$10, 40, 160, 640$$

   A. 2560, 10240, 40960

   B. 10240, 40960, 163840,

   C. 10, 40, 160

   D. 640, 2560, 10240

**Answer:**

**QUESTION 35**

Given f(x) = 5x + 20 and g(x) = 6x + 12, what is f(g(3))?

   A. 30

   B. 35

   C. 170

   D. 222

**Answer:**

**QUESTION 36**

In his algebra class, John's professor assigns 3 group projects and 3 exams. The three group projects are worth 20%, 25%, and 20%, respectively, of the final course grade. The three exams are worth 10%, 15%, and 10% of the final course grade. If John earned a 73, 75, and 97 on the group projects, respectively, and a 99, 93, and 100 on the exams, respectively, then what is his final course grade?

   A. 91.3

   B. 89.5

   C. 86.6

   D. 78.2

**Answer:**

**QUESTION 37**

The owner of a local gym asked people in the community how many hours they work out during the week. The owner recorded his results in the line plot below. What is the median, mode, and range of the data set?

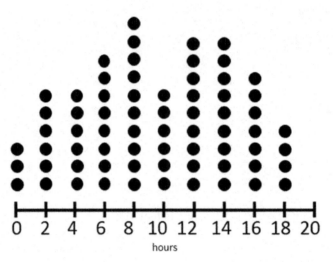

A. Median = 8; Mode = 10; Range =20

B. Median = 9; Mode = 8; Range = 18

C. Median = 10; Mode = 8; Range = 1

D. Median = 16; Mode = 10; Range = 16

**Answer:**

**QUESTION 38**

What of the following scenarios can be modeled by the line graph shown below?

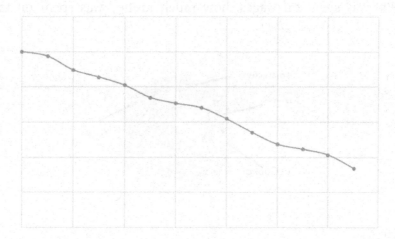

A. At the end of every year, Marcus takes his car to the dealership. The mechanic at the dealership performs the annual check-ups and tells Marcus the market value of the car. Marcus takes the value of the car at the end of each year and creates a line graph.

B. Michael takes out a loan from a bank. He pays off equal portions of the loan every month. Michael wants to create a line graph that shows the value of loan he had remaining at the end of each month that he made a payment in.

C. Maria takes out a loan from a bank. She pays off equal portions of the loan every month. Maria wants to create a line graph that shows the cumulative sum of money she has given to the bank at the end of each month.

D. A and B

**Answer:**

## QUESTION 39

The following pie chart breaks down several of the expenses for a grocery store in a given year. If a total of $923,800 was spent on wages, how much money was spent on taxes and physical capital?

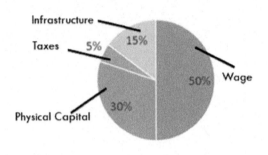

A. $1,847,600

B. $646,660

C. $554,280

D. $92,380

**Answer:**

## QUESTION 40

Marissa's neighbors have 3 dogs. What is the probability that two of the three dogs are male?

A. 0.875

B. 0.500

C. 0.375

D. 0.250

**Answer:**

**QUESTION 41**

Of the four options below, which data shown can be a possible probability distribution?

A.

| Y | -5 | 4 | 3 | 2 | 1 |
|---|---|---|---|---|---|
| P(Y) | 0 | 0.1 | 0.4 | 0.3 | 0.2 |

B.

| Y | 5 | 4 | 3 | 2 | 1 |
|---|---|---|---|---|---|
| P(Y) | 0 | 0.2 | 0.5 | 0.3 | 0.2 |

C.

| Y | A | B | C | D | E |
|---|---|---|---|---|---|
| P(Y) | -0.1 | 0.2 | 0.4 | 0.3 | 0.2 |

D.

| Y | A | B | C | D | E |
|---|---|---|---|---|---|
| P(Y) | 0 | 0.1 | 0.4 | 0.2 | 0.2 |

**Answer:**

**QUESTION 42**

Find the value of:

$$\frac{5! \times 6! \times 8!}{10! \times 2! \times 0!}$$

A. 480

B. 690

C. 12

D. undefined

**Answer:**

**QUESTION 43**

What is the sum of the interior angles of a nonagon?

**Answer:**

**QUESTION 44**

If points ABCD are connected to form a rectangle, what is the area of this rectangle?

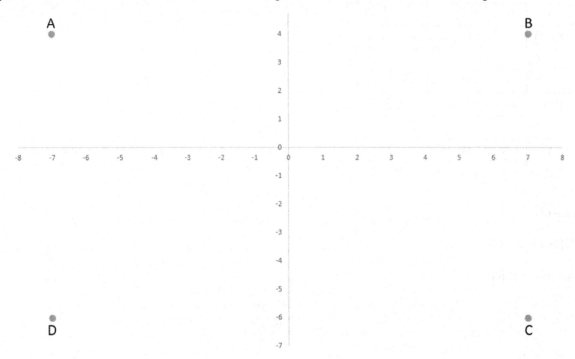

    A. 140 feet

    B. 48 feet

    C. 42 feet

    D. 0 feet

**Answer:**

## QUESTION 45

The location of four kids playing at a park can be plotted on a Cartesian coordinate xy-plane. The first kid is at Point A. The second kid is at Point B. The third kid is at Point C. If the fourth kid is in the middle of the first and third kid, then how far is the fourth kid from the second kid?

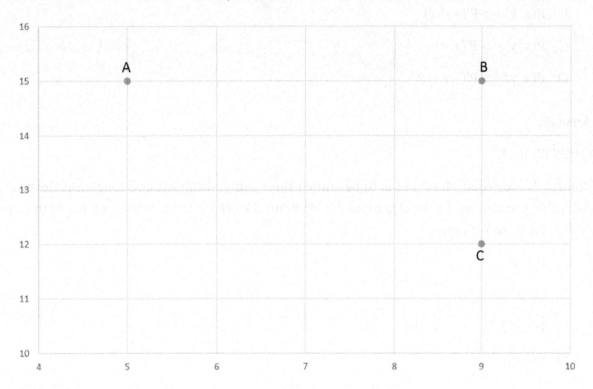

A. 2.5

B. 3

C. 4

D. 5

**Answer:**

## QUESTION 46

Which of the following reflections is done across the line $y = -x$?

    A.  $P(x, y) \rightarrow P'(x, -y)$

    B.  $P(x, y) \rightarrow P'(-x, y)$

    C.  $P(x, y) \rightarrow P'(y, x)$

    D.  $P(x, y) \rightarrow P'(-y, -x)$

**Answer:**

## QUESTION 47

Point A is located at (4, 6) and is to be shifted three units to the left and four units downward. After this translation, the point is rotated 270° about the origin. What is the location of this point after these transformations?

    A.  (2, -1)

    B.  (1, 2)

    C.  (-1, -2)

    D.  (-2, 1)

**Answer:**

# QUESTION 48

Which of the following histograms displays data that is right skewed?

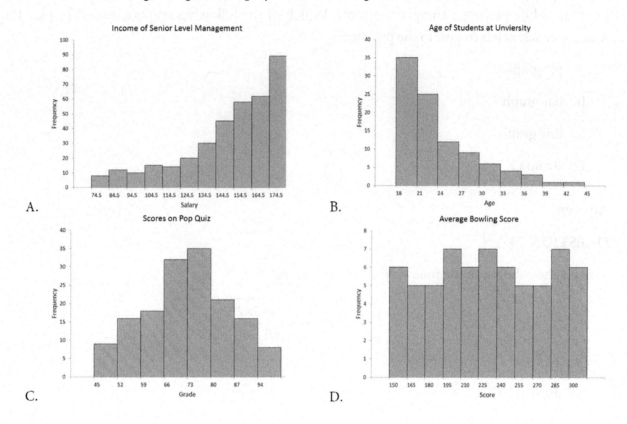

A.

B.

C.

D.

**Answer:**

## QUESTION 49

A principal asked the high school coach for the number of injuries students suffered in the past ten years while playing a competitive sport. Which of the following graph(s) would display the data the coach needs to give to the principal?

    A. pie graph

    B. bar graph

    C. line graph

    D. B and C

**Answer:**

## QUESTION 50

What is the solution to the following set of operations?

$$\left(\frac{5}{4}\right)^{-2} \times 5^3 \times \frac{\sqrt{18\times2+3\times2^2}}{80}$$

    A. $4\sqrt{3}$

    B. $3\sqrt{3}$

    C. $3\sqrt{4}$

    D. $4\sqrt{16}$

**Answer:**

## QUESTION 51

Which of the following is NOT equivalent to the radical below?

$$\sqrt[3]{324}$$

    A. $3 \times \sqrt[3]{12}$

    B. $\left(\frac{1}{324}\right)^{-\frac{1}{3}}$

    C. $\left((324)^2\right)^{\frac{1}{6}}$

    D. 18

**Answer:**

**QUESTION 52**

Which of the following options is not true?

A. Examples of real numbers are: $0.7458, \frac{1}{2}, -4.254, 0, 1, 5.254, -\sqrt{2.254}$

B. Examples of whole numbers are: $0, 2, \frac{4}{2}, \sqrt{25}, 100$

C. Example of irrational numbers: $\sqrt{23}, \pi, \sqrt{2}, \sqrt{-25}$

D. Examples of natural numbers: $1, 2, 3, 28, 45897$

**Answer:**

**QUESTION 53**

For a charity event, a basket was passed around, and people were asked to place any amount of money they desired into the basket. Jerry was the first person to receive the basket and he put in $100. Jacob was the next person and he decided to place 26% of what he saw in the basket. Timmy was the third recipient of the basket and he decided to place 125% of what he saw in the basket. Maria received the basket next and she placed $20 into the basket. Bob received the basket next and he placed 0.05% of what he saw in the basket. Bob's wife saw the basket next, and she placed 150% of what she in the basket. How much money has accumulated in the basket so far?

A. $421.02

B. $630.75

C. $759.13

D. $796.69

**Answer:**

**QUESTION 54**

At an athletic department store, the ratio of basketball jerseys to baseball jerseys is 8 to 3, and the ratio of football jerseys to soccer jerseys is 1 to 5. If the ratio of baseball jerseys to soccer jerseys is 7 to 4 and there are a total of 350 basketball jerseys, then how many football jerseys are at the store?

    A. 15

    B. 375

    C. 2000

    D. 350

**Answer:**

**QUESTION 55**

Which of the following answer choices contains a prime number, a composite number, an odd number, an even number, a factor of 126, a multiple of 7, and a number divisible by 36? Furthermore, the answer choice should contain 7 unique numbers and be arranged in order from least to greatest.

    A. {3, 9, 13, 16, 21, 35, 72}

    B. {1, 6, 7, 13, 21, 35, 108}

    C. {11, 15, 13, 18, 32, 49, 36}

    D. {13, 25, 30, 252, 700, 3600}

**Answer:**

# Middle School Practice Exam Answers – Test 1

| Question Number | Selected Answer | Question Number | Selected Answer |
|:---:|:---:|:---:|:---:|
| 1 | A | 31 | B |
| 2 | C | 32 | D |
| 3 | 0.667 | 33 | B |
| 4 | B | 34 | A |
| 5 | B | 35 | C |
| 6 | C | 36 | C |
| 7 | C | 37 | B |
| 8 | B | 38 | A |
| 9 | C | 39 | B |
| 10 | B | 40 | D |
| 11 | 100 | 41 | A |
| 12 | B | 42 | A |
| 13 | C | 43 | 1260 |
| 14 | D | 44 | A |
| 15 | C | 45 | A |
| 16 | C | 46 | D |
| 17 | D | 47 | A |
| 18 | D | 48 | B |
| 19 | D | 49 | D |
| 20 | A | 50 | A |
| 21 | A | 51 | D |
| 22 | C | 52 | C |
| 23 | B | 53 | C |
| 24 | B | 54 | A |
| 25 | B | 55 | A |
| 26 | D | | |
| 27 | A | | |
| 28 | 125 | | |
| 29 | A | | |
| 30 | B | | |

NOTE: Getting approximately 80% of the questions correct increases chances of obtaining passing score on the real exam. This varies from different states and university programs.

This page is intentionally left blank.

**QUESTION 1**

At a high school, the ratio of basketball players to baseball players is 7 to 3, and the ratio of football players to soccer players is 8 to 5. If the ratio of baseball players to soccer players is 1 to 4, then what is the ratio of the basketball players to football players?

A. $\frac{35}{96}$

B. $\frac{7}{8}$

C. $\frac{7}{24}$

D. $\frac{18}{35}$

**Answer:** A

**Explanation:** The best approach is to write the ratios in fraction form; this is shown below

$$\frac{\text{basketball}}{\text{baseball}} = \frac{7}{3}, \frac{\text{football}}{\text{soccer}} = \frac{8}{5}, \frac{\text{baseball}}{\text{soccer}} = \frac{1}{4}$$

To find the ratio of basketball players to the football players, the ratio of basketball players to baseball players needs to be multiplied by the ratio of baseball players to soccer players. Then, the result needs to be multiplied by the inverse of the ratio of football players to soccer players. These operations are summarized below:

$$\frac{\text{basketball}}{\text{baseball}} \times \frac{\text{baseball}}{\text{soccer}} \times \frac{\text{soccer}}{\text{football}}$$

$$\frac{7}{3} \times \frac{1}{4} \times \frac{5}{8} = \frac{35}{96}$$

The result of the operations shows that the ratio of basketball players to football players is $\frac{35}{96}$.

## QUESTION 2

If the value in the thousands place of the first number is multiplied with the value in the hundreds place in the second number, and this product is added to the value in the thousandths place of the third number, then what number will result from these operations?

Number 1: 124,587

Number 2: 25,478.2445

Number 3: 145.25402

A. 39

B. 35

C. 20

D. 16

**Answer:** C

**Explanation:** The first number has 6 digits. The digit in the thousands place is the value 4 places to the left of the decimal point. The first number does not have a decimal point, so it is assumed to be at the end of the number. Thus, the value in the thousands place of the first number is 4. The second number has 5 digits to the left of the decimal point and 4 digits to the right of the decimal point. The digit in the hundreds place is the value 3 places to the left of the decimal point. Thus, the value in the hundreds place of the second number is 4. The first operation to be performed is the multiplication of the value in the thousands place of the first number and the value in the hundreds place in the second number. This operation results in 4 x 4 =16. The second operation required the addition of 16 and the value in the thousandths place of the third number. The third number has 3 digits to the left of the decimal point and 5 digits to the right of the decimal point. The thousandths place is the value 3 places to the right of the decimal point. Thus, the value in the thousandths place of the third number is 4. The addition of 4 to 16 results in 20.

## QUESTION 3

Fifteen people are waiting for the winning numbers for the daily lottery. The age and gender of the 15 people are given below. If there will be a winner among the fifteen people, what is the probability that the winner will be a female or an individual younger than 25?

| Gender | M | F | F | M | M | M | F | F | M | M | F | M | F | F | M |
|--------|---|---|---|---|---|---|---|---|---|---|---|---|---|---|---|
| Age | 24 | 26 | 18 | 18 | 26 | 22 | 24 | 21 | 19 | 25 | 26 | 24 | 32 | 35 | 41 |

**Answer:** 0.667

**Explanation:** The first step is to determine the total number of females in the group of 15 people; this number is 7. The next step is to determine, which of the remaining 7 people are younger than 25; this number is 3. Thus, there are a total of 10 people who are either female or younger than 25. The probability that one of these ten people is the lottery winner among the 15 people is 10/15=0.667.

5 + 7 = 12

## QUESTION 4

If the value of t, in the equation below, is increased by 2, how will the value of g change?

$$g = 4 \times (t + 2)^2 + 3 \times (t+p) - 5$$

A.  25

B.  16t + 54

C.  16t + 4p + 54

D.  54

**Answer:** B

**Explanation:** The best approach to this problem is to first expand the equation given. The expansion results in the following expression:

$$g = 4 \times (t + 2)^2 + 3 \times (t+p) - 5 = 4t^2 + 19t + 3p + 11$$

The next step is to input (t+2) for the variable t in the expression above. This results in the following:

$$g = 4t^2 + 19t + 3p + 11 = 4(t + 2)^2 + 19(t + 2) + 3p + 11 = 4t^2 + 35t + 3p + 65$$

The final step is to subtract the original expression obtained from the new expression to see the effect of adding 2 to the value of t. This is shown below:

$$(4t^2 + 35t + 3p + 65) - (4t^2 + 19t + 3p + 11) = 16t + 54$$

**QUESTION 5**

The position of a particle moving in an accelerator is given by $p(t) = 2t^3 - 4t^2 + 2t - 1$. What is the position of the particle at $t = 4$ seconds?

    A.  23

    B.  43

    C.  71

    D.  7943

**Answer:** B

**Explanation:** The answer will come after substituting 4 for the variable t in the formula for the position.

$$p(2) = 2 \times (4^3) - 4 \times (4^2) + 2 \times (4) - 1 = 2 \times (64) - 4 \times (16) + 2 \times (4) - 1 = 128 - 64 + 8 - 1 = 71$$

## QUESTION 6

Two trapezoids are shown in the figure below. Trapezoid 1 has height of 8 in, a base of 10 in, and an area of 148 in². Trapezoid 2 has height of 16 in and a base of 20 in. If the two trapezoids are similar, what is the length of the other base in Trapezoid 2?

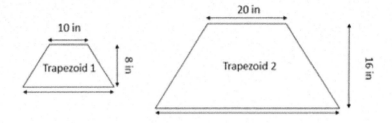

A. 12 in

B. 27 in

C. 54 in

D. Not enough information

**Answer:** C

**Explanation:** To determine the length of the second base in Trapezoid 2, its area needs to be calculated. Since the two trapezoids are similar, its area will be determined by taking into account the ratios between the side lengths of the two trapezoids. The ratio of the areas of two similar polygons equals the square of the ratios of the lengths of any two corresponding sides. The lengths of the top bases of each trapezoid can be used to determine the ratio of the areas of the two trapezoids, as shown below.

$$\frac{A_{T1}}{A_{T2}} = \left(\frac{10}{20}\right)^2 = \frac{1}{4}$$

The area of Trapezoid 2 will be 4 times the area of Trapezoid 1; this is calculated to be 592 inches². With the area of Trapezoid 2 known, along with the length of the height and one base, the length of the other base can be calculated, as shown below.

$$A_{T2} = \frac{1}{2} \times h \times (b_1 + b_2) = 592 = \frac{1}{2} \times 16 \times (20 + b_2) \rightarrow b_2 = 54 \text{ inches}$$

## QUESTION 7

In the figure below, angle A is equal to x – 24 degrees. If angle B is equal to x – 36 degrees, then what is the value of x?

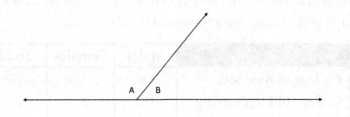

A. 84°

B. 86°

C. 120°

D. 180°

**Answer:** C

**Explanation:** The figure shows the sum of angles A and B must equal 180 degrees. To solve this problem, the given values of angles A, and B are added and set equal to 180°. This creates an equation with one unknown variable, which can be solved for.

$$\angle A + \angle B = x - 24 + x - 36 = 2x - 60 = 180° \rightarrow x = 120°$$

## QUESTION 8

A university counselor was asked to report on the number of students enrolled in the five different colleges at the university. The counselor was asked to also report on the number of males and females in each of those five colleges. The data the counselor obtained is shown below. Which of the following graphs accurately represent the data obtained?

|  | Males | Females | Total |
|---|---|---|---|
| **College of Business** | 250 | 300 | 550 |
| **College of Engineering** | 162 | 85 | 247 |
| **College of Liberal Arts** | 144 | 225 | 369 |
| **College of Natural Sciences** | 325 | 336 | 661 |
| **College of Technology** | 114 | 96 | 210 |

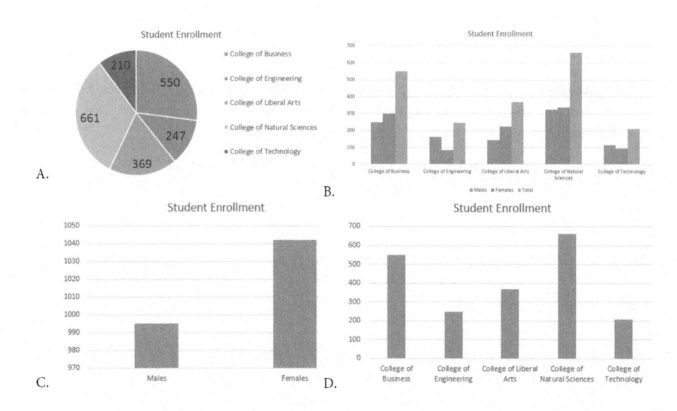

**Answer:** B

**Explanation:** The counselor is asked to report on data that can be broken down into qualitative categories, so the best representation of the data will be a bar graph. Since the counselor was asked to report on the total enrollment in each college and also the distribution of the enrollment size by gender, the best representation is shown in option B. Option B is corect because anyone viewing the graph can read the total number of students in each college and also the number of males and females in each college. The other options do not convey these three sets of information all at once.

## QUESTION 9

One letter will be randomly selected from the set below. What is the probability that is a vowel or precedes the letter G in alphabetical order?

$$\{A, B, C, L, M, N, O, P, E, F, H, I, T, S, V, U\}$$

A. 0.0977

B. 0.3125

C. 0.5000

D. 0.6250

**Answer:** C

**Explanation:** There are a total of 16 letters given in the set. Of the 16 letters, 5 are vowels. Thus, the probability of selecting a vowel is $\frac{5}{16} = 0.3125$. Of the 16 letters, 5 letters precede the letter G, and, of these 5 letters, only 3 are not vowels. Thus, the probability of selecting a letter that precedes the letter G is $\frac{3}{16}=0.1875$. The probability of either of these events occurring is 0.3125 + 0.1875=0.50.

NOTE: Only three of the five letters preceding letter G are considered because the other 2 are represented in the probability of selecting a vowel.

## QUESTION 10

Considering the Venn diagram below, which of the following options is true?

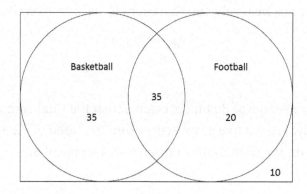

A. P(Basketball) < P(Football)

B. P(Basketball and Football) < P(Football)

C. P(Basketball and Football) > P(Basketball)

D. P(Basketball or Football) = 1.00

**Answer:** B

**Explanation:** To answer this question, each of the answer choices needs to be evaluated.

In option A, it is stated that the probability of football is greater than the probability of basketball. However, the probability of basketball is 0.70 and the probability of football is 0.55; which contradicts the statement in option A.

In option B, it is stated that the probability of basketball and football is greater than the probability of football. The probability of basketball and football is 0.35, and the probability of football is 0.55. This option is true.

In option C, it is stated that the probability of basketball and football is greater than the probability of basketball. The probability of basketball and football is 0.35, and the probability of basketball is 0.70. This option is not true.

In option D, it is stated the probability of basketball or football is equal to 1.00. This not true because the probability of basketball or football is equal to 0.70 + 0.55 − 0.35=0.90.

**QUESTION 11**

Jacob received the following scores on his first five exams. If there is one more exam Jacob needs to take, then what grade must he receive on that exam to have an overall average of 80?

72, 68, 91, 54, 95

**Answer:** 100

**Explanation:** To have an average of 80 on six exams, then the total sum of the scores must equal to 480 ($80 \times 6$). Currently, Jacob's five exam scores sum to a total of $72 + 68 + 91 + 54 + 95 = 380$, so he must receive a 100 on the sixth exam to receive an average of 80.

**QUESTION 12**

Ronald, George and James have each ordered a pizza. Ronald's pizza is 30% larger than George's pizza. James' pizza is 30% larger than George's pizza. Ronald has eaten 37.5% of his pizza. George has about 0.05 of his pizza remaining. James has eaten $\frac{3}{7}$ of his pizza. Approximately, which of the following correctly orders who has eaten the most pizza?

    A. Ronald > James > George

    B. George > James > Ronald

    C. James > George> Ronald

    D. Ronald > George > James

**Answer:** B

**Explanation:**

The best approach to this problem is to assume that the size of George's pizza is x.

    Ronald's pizza is 30% larger than George's pizza, so the size of his pizza is 1.3x.

    James' pizza is 30% larger than George's pizza, so the size of his pizza is 1.3x.

Now that the size of each person's pizza is known, the next approach is to determine the amount of pizza each has eaten.

    The problem statement says Ronald has eaten 37.5% of his pizza, so he has eaten a total of 1.3x × 37.5% = 0.4875x.

    The problem statement says George has 0.05 of his pizza remaining, so he has eaten a total of x – 0.05x = 0.95x.

    The problem statement says James has eaten $\frac{3}{7}$ of his pizza, so he has eaten a total of 1.3x $\times \frac{3}{7} = 0.557$x.

George has eaten the most pizza, and Ronald has eaten the least, so the correct answer is B.

## QUESTION 13

Set S contains the following numbers. Which of the following options lists the rational numbers of the set in order from least to greatest?

$$S = \{-1.25 \times 10^{-4}, 5.2 \times 10^{3}, 0.111, 1.75, \sqrt{2}, \sqrt{-25}, \sqrt{4}, \sqrt{25}, 1.25 \times 10^{-5}, 125478, 145\sqrt{2}, \sqrt{5.2 \times 10^{3}}\}$$

A. $\{\sqrt{-25}, -1.25 \times 10^{-4}, 1.25 \times 10^{-5}, 0.111, 1.75, \sqrt{4}, \sqrt{25}, \sqrt{5.2 \times 10^{3}}, 5.2 \times 10^{3}, 125478\}$

B. $\{-1.25 \times 10^{-4}, 1.25 \times 10^{-5}, 0.111, 1.75, \sqrt{2}, \sqrt{4}, \sqrt{25}, \sqrt{5.2 \times 10^{3}}, 5.2 \times 10^{3}, 125478\}$

C. $\{-1.25 \times 10^{-4}, 1.25 \times 10^{-5}, 0.111, 1.75, \sqrt{4}, \sqrt{25}, \sqrt{5.2 \times 10^{3}}, 5.2 \times 10^{3}, 125478\}$

D. $\{1.25 \times 10^{-5}, -1.25 \times 10^{-4}, 0.111, 1.75, \sqrt{4}, \sqrt{25}, \sqrt{5.2 \times 10^{3}}, 5.2 \times 10^{3}, 125478\}$

**Answer:** C

**Explanation:** The first step is to distinguish which of the numbers in the set are rational numbers and which are not. The rational numbers are:

$$\{-1.25 \times 10^{-4}, 5.2 \times 10^{3}, 0.111, 1.75, \sqrt{4}, \sqrt{25}, 1.25 \times 10^{-5}, 125478, \sqrt{5.2 \times 10^{3}}\}$$

This automatically proves that options A and B are incorrect.

The next step is to arrange the selected numbers from least to greatest. The result is shown below

$$\{-1.25 \times 10^{-4}, 1.25 \times 10^{-5}, 0.111, 1.75, \sqrt{4}, \sqrt{25}, \sqrt{5.2 \times 10^{3}}, 5.2 \times 10^{3}, 125478\}$$

# QUESTION 14

A bucket consists of red and blue marbles. The red marbles weigh 2 grams and the blue marble weigh 7 grams. The total weight of the bucket is 85 grams. If it is known that there are 2 more red marbles than blue marbles, then what is the total number of marbles in the bucket?

    A. 8

    B. 9

    C. 18

    D. 20

**Answer:** D

**Explanation:** This problem requires setting up a system of equations that model the number of marbles in the bucket and the weight of the bucket.

The number of red marbles can be defined with variable $r$. The number of blue marbles can be defined with variable $b$. The total number of marbles is $r + b$. It is known that there are 2 more red marbles than blue marbles, so $r = 2 + b$.

The weight of single red marble is 2 grams, so the weight of $r$ red marbles is $2r$. The weight of a single blue marble is 7 grams, so the weight of $b$ blue marbles is $7b$. The total weight of $b$ blue marbles and $r$ red marbles can be defined as $7b + 2r$. The problem states that the total weight of the marbles is 85 grams, so the total weight can be expressed as $7b + 2r = 85$. Substituting the expression of $r = 2 + b$ into $7b + 2r = 85$ can yield the value of $b$. The substitution results in $7b + 2(2 + b) = 85$, which yields a value of 9 for $b$.

$$7b + 4 + 2b = 85$$

$$9b = 81$$

$$b = 9$$

The analysis above yields a total number of 9 blue marbles and 11 red marbles. There are a total of 20 marbles.

## QUESTION 15

At time 0, Chris leaves work and heads home. The following graphs shows the distance Chris is from work as time goes by. During the period between 1 and 5 minutes, which of the following best describes what Chris was doing?

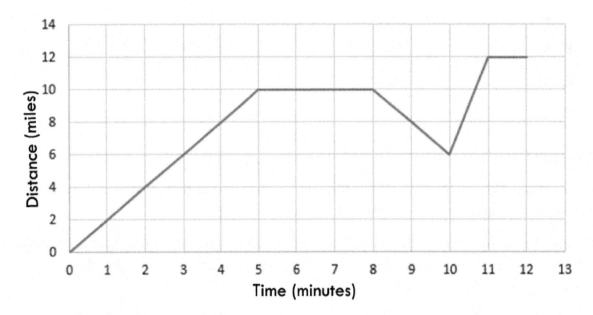

A. Chris is stuck in traffic and is not moving.

B. Chris is heading in a direction towards his workplace.

C. Chris is heading home at a constant speed.

D. Chris has parked his car in his driveway.

**Answer:** C

**Explanation:** Between 1 and 5 minutes, the line modeling his distance with respect to time changes constantly. This line implies a constant change in distance with respect to time. Since the ratio of distance to time is considered to be the speed, the line implies he is heading home at a constant speed. Option C is correct.

**QUESTION 16**

Which of the given equations has the following three zeros and passes through the x values below?

$$x = -1, x = 2, \text{ and } x = -6$$

    A.  $f(x) = x^2 - x - 2$

    B.  $f(x) = 2x - x^2$

    C.  $f(x) = 2x^3 + 10x^2 - 16x - 24$

    D.  $f(x) = x^3 - 7x^2 + 4x + 12$

**Answer:** C

**Explanation:** The problem gives three zeros of a function, which implies the function is a cubic function. This eliminates answer choices A and B. When solving for the zeros of a polynomial, the polynomial is usually factored and each factor is set to equal zero. In this problem, the zeros are already given, so it is best to work backwards.

    $x = -1$ implies that the equation has a factor of $(x + 1)$ because $x + 1 = 0$ results in $x = -1$

    $x = 2$ implies that the equation has a factor of $(x - 2)$ because $x - 2 = 0$ results in $x = 2$

    $x = -6$ implies that the equation has a factor of $(x + 6)$ because $x + 6 = 0$ results in $x = -6$

The three factors of the cubic function can be used to obtain the general form of the family of cubic functions that have the zeros given in the problem statement. The three given zeros can be used only to obtain the general solution because any constant factor can be multiplied to each term in the equation and still result in the same zeros. The general form of the family of cubic functions that results from multiplying the three factors is shown below. Only answer choice C can belong in this family. Answer choice C is the result of multiplying the general form by a value of 2. Answer choice D is not a member of this family.

$$(x + 1) \times (x - 2) = x^2 - x - 2$$

$$(x^2 - x - 2) \times (x + 6) = x^3 + 5x^2 - 8x - 12$$

General form of the family of cubic functions: $a \times (x^3 + 5x^2 - 8x - 12)$

where a is any non-zero number

**QUESTION 17**

How many zeros does the function in the graph below show?

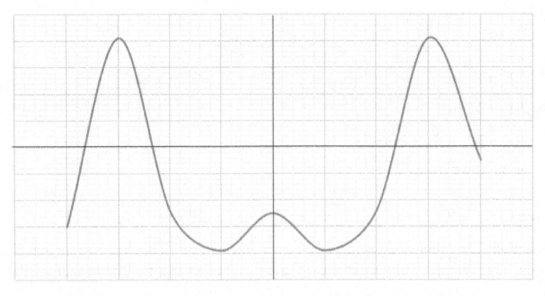

    A. 1

    B. 2

    C. 3

    D. 4

**Answer:** D

**Explanation:** The zeros of a function are the x-coordinate values when a function crosses the x axis. In the graph shown above, the function crosses the x-axis for a total of 4 times. Thus, the correct answer is D.

**QUESTION 18**

Select the answer choice that does NOT equal to the following rational expression:

$$\frac{m^2 + 9m + 18}{m^2 - m - 12}$$

A. $\dfrac{(m+3) \times (m+6)}{(m-4) \times (m+3)}$

B. $\dfrac{(m+6)}{(m-4)}$

C. $\dfrac{m^2 + 18 + 9m}{m^2 - 12 - m}$

D. $\left(\dfrac{m^2 + 9m + 18}{m^2 - m - 12}\right)^{-1}$

**Answer:** D

**Explanation:** To answer this question, it is necessary to factor the numerator and denominator, and then simplify the expression step by step. The numerator $(m^2+9m+18)$ can be factored into $(m + 3) (m + 6)$. The denominator $(m^2 - m - 12)$ can be factored into $(m – 4) (m + 3)$.

Answer choice A is an expression equivalent to the original expression given because its numerator and denominator are simply factors of the numerator and denominator in the original expression.

Answer choice B is an expression equivalent to the original expression given because its numerator and denominator consists of the factors in the numerator and denominator in the original expression except for the $(m + 3)$, which has been removed since it appears in both the numerator and denominator.

Answer choice C is an expression equivalent to the original expression. The only change that has occurred is a rearrangement of the order in which the terms appear in the numerator and denominator, and this does not affect the value of the expression.

Answer choice D is an expression that is NOT equivalent to the original expression. The expression inside the parenthesis is equivalent to the expression originally given, but the expression in the parenthesis is raised to a -1 one exponent. This causes the entire expression inside to flip, which does not result in an equivalent form of the expression originally given.

## QUESTION 19

Which of the following options is false?

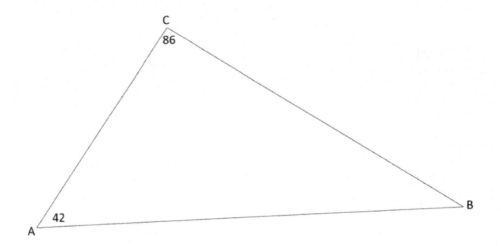

    A. ∢CAB <∢CBA <∢BCA

    B. $\overline{BC}$< $\overline{CA}$<$\overline{BA}$

    C. ∢CAB + ∢CBA + ∢BCA = 180

    D. $\overline{BA}$>$\overline{BC}$>$\overline{CA}$

**Answer:** D

**Explanation:** The best approach to this problem is to evaluate each option given

The first option requires knowledge of all three angles. Only two angles are given, so the third angle must be calculated. Knowing that the sum of three angles of a triangle adds to 180°, the known angles can be subtracted from 180°. This results in a value of 52° for the third angle. With three angles known, it becomes obvious that ∢CAB <∢CBA <∢BCA.

If the three angles are known, then the relative sizes of the three sides can be determined. The largest side of a triangle is opposite the largest angle of the triangle. The smallest side of a triangle is opposite the smallest angle of the triangle. With these two properties, it can be deduced that side BA is the largest and side BC is the smallest. This proves that option B is true.

As stated earlier, all three angles of a triangle sum to 180°, so this option is true.

Option D is false for the same reason that option B is true.

**QUESTION 20**

A chair manufacturer can build a maximum of 200 chairs in one month. The manufacturer takes orders of 5 chairs per order. For the month of March, the manufacturer has already secured orders for a total of 120 chairs. What is the maximum number of orders the manufacturer can add to the production for March?

    A. 16

    B. 40

    C. 80

    D. 120

**Answer:** A

**Explanation:** Since the manufacturer has secured orders for 120 chairs, the manufacturer can take orders for up to 80 more chairs as 200 − 120=80. With each order having 5 chairs, the number of orders the manufacture can take is 80 ÷ 5 =16.

**QUESTION 21**

Which number line below graphically represents the answer to the following inequality?

$$|4x + 12| < 2x + 12$$

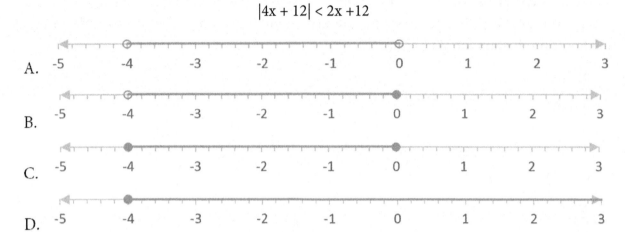

A.

B.

C.

D.

**Answer:** A

**Explanation:** To solve an inequality of the form $|x| < a$, the absolute value signs are removed and the following inequality is solved: $-a < x < a$. The left portion is solved: $-a < x$. The right portion is solved as $x < a$.

$|4x + 12| < 2x + 12$ becomes $-2x - 12 < 4x + 12 < 2x + 12$.

$4x + 12 < 2x + 12$ becomes $-2x - 12 + 12 - 4x < 4x + 12 + 12 - 4x$ which is equivalent to $-6x < 24$, resulting in $x > -4$

$4x + 12 < 2x + 12$ becomes $4x + 12 - 12 - 2x < 2x + 12 - 12 - 2x$ which is equivalent to $2x < 0$, resulting in $x < 0$

The answer to the inequality becomes $-4 < x < 0$. This inequality is depicted in the number line for answer A. Also, answer options B, C, and D can be discarded since they have closed dots at the end points. Closed dots represents symbols of $\leq$ and $\geq$.

**QUESTION 22**

Which of the following options is a median for the isosceles triangle shown below?

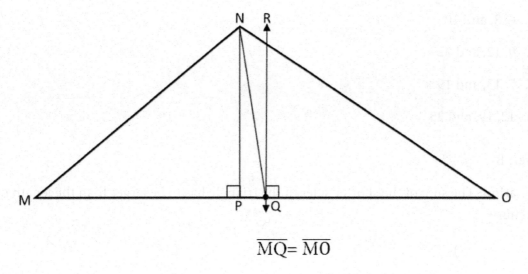

$$\overline{MQ} = \overline{MO}$$

A. $\overline{NP}$

B. $\overleftrightarrow{RQ}$

C. $\overline{NQ}$

D. $\overline{MQ}$

**Answer:** C

**Explanation:** The median is defined as the line segment that connects a vertex to the midpoint of the side opposite the vertex. In this figure, N is a vertex, and the midpoint on the opposite side is Q. The line segment $\overline{NQ}$ is a median from N to the middle of $\overline{MO}$.

**QUESTION 23**

Which of the following sets of numbers cannot be the measurements of the sides of a triangle?

    A.  6, 8, and 10

    B.  9, 12, and 22

    C.  7, 13, and 19

    D.  12, 19, and 25

**Answer:** B

**Explanation:** The sum of the shorter sides of the triangle has to be larger than the length of the hypotenuse.

**QUESTION 24**

John has been told by his parents that he can no longer spend more than $100 per month. In the first week of the month, John spent $14 on a movie ticket. In the second week, John spend $12 at the arcade. In the third week, John chose not to spend any money, so he could spend more the following week at his friend's birthday party. Which of the following number lines most accurately shows how much money John can spend in the last week of the month?

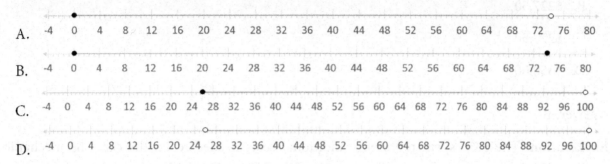

A.  -4  0  4  8  12  16  20  24  28  32  36  40  44  48  52  56  60  64  68  72  76  80

B.  -4  0  4  8  12  16  20  24  28  32  36  40  44  48  52  56  60  64  68  72  76  80

C.  -4  0  4  8  12  16  20  24  28  32  36  40  44  48  52  56  60  64  68  72  76  80  84  88  92  96  100

D.  -4  0  4  8  12  16  20  24  28  32  36  40  44  48  52  56  60  64  68  72  76  80  84  88  92  96  100

**Answer:** B

**Explanation:** Of the $100 restriction on his monthly expenditures, John has spent $14 the first week, $12 the second week, and $0 the third week. These three expenditures sum to a total value of $26, which results in $74 remaining in his total monthly budget. To ensure that John does not exceed his monthly restriction, John can spend anywhere between $0 and $74, as depicted in the number line shown in answer choice B.

Option B is chosen over Option A because Option B allows for John to spend $74, which would not exceed his budget. However, Option A only allows John to spent up $74 not $74.

**QUESTION 25**

A mechanic charges $50 an hour to fix a car and requires 65% reimbursement of any additional costs needed to fix the car. If the mechanic had to purchase $350 worth of the equipment to fix the car, how much of this cost will be paid back to the mechanic.

  A. $122.50

  B. $227.50

  C. $277.50

  D. $350.00

**Answer:** B

**Explanation:** The $350 spent represents additional costs needed to fix the car. The mechanic requires 65% of the costs to be reimbursed. 65% of the $350 is $227.50.

$$\frac{65}{100} \times 350 = 227.50$$

## QUESTION 26

If a < b < - 1 < 0 < 1 < c < d, then which of the following fractions has the smallest value?

A. $\dfrac{b}{a}$

B. $\dfrac{c}{d}$

C. $\dfrac{0}{c}$

D. $\dfrac{d}{b}$

**Answer:** D

**Explanation:** To solve this problem, the best approach is to analyze each option.

In option A, two negative numbers are being divided, so the result will be a positive number.

In option B, two positive numbers are being divided, so the result will be a positive number.

In option C, the numerator has a 0, so the result is 0.

In option D, a positive number is being divided by a negative number, so the result is a negative number.

Without knowing the magnitude of any of the values, it is certain option D will have the smallest value because it results in a negative number.

**QUESTION 27**

What digit will be in the hundreds place of 1.25468 x $10^{25}$?

    A.  0

    B.  6

    C.  5

    D.  2

**Answer:** A

**Explanation:** In this problem, the number is represented in scientific notation. If the scientific notation was to be expanded to standard notation, the decimal place would move to the right 25 times. In front of the decimal, there will be 20 zeroes and the digits 125468. Since, the digit in the hundreds place is the value 3 units to the left of the decimal point; the hundred place for this number will be a zero.

**QUESTION 28**

In parallelogram MNOP, $\angle M = x + 15$ and $\angle N = 3x + 5$. What is the value of $\angle P$?

**Answer:** 125

**Explanation:** In a parallelogram, corresponding angles are supplementary and opposite angles are equivalent. Thus, $\angle M$ and $\angle N$ are supplementary and $\angle N$ is equivalent to $\angle P$. The known information about angles M and N can be used to find the value of $\angle N$, which will be equivalent to $\angle P$.

The sum of angles M and N is equal to $4x + 20$, which is equivalent to 180. Solving for x yield a value of $x = 40$. Using this value of x in the definition of angle N yields a value of 125. Thus, angle P has a value of 125.

## QUESTION 29

What is the result of performing this multiplication?

$$(-15 + 3i) \times (5 + 4i)$$

    A.   -87 – 45i

    B.   -87 – 33i

    C.   -63 – 45i

    D.   -63 – 33i

**Answer:** A

**Explanation:** The best approach is to first expand the multiplication out by multiplying each term with one another. The result of this is shown below. It is important to note that $i \times i = -1$. After multiplying each term, the results are simplified, also shown below.

$$-15 \times 5 + -15 \times 4i + 3i \times 5 + 3i \times 4i = -75 + -60i + 15i -12 = -87 – 45i$$

## QUESTION 30

What value(s) of x will satisfy the following equation?

$$18x^2 + 24x + 8 = 0$$

A.  0

B.  -2/3

C.  2/3

D.  2/3 and -2/3

**Answer:** B

**Explanation:** The best approach to this problem is to use the quadratic formula, which is shown below. In the quadratic formula, the variables a, b, and c correspond to the standard form of a quadratic equation: $ax^2 + bx + c = 0$. In this problem a = 18, b = 24, and c = 8. When these values are inserted into the quadratic formula, x = -2/3.

$$x = \frac{-b \pm \sqrt{b^2 - 4ac}}{2a}$$

$$x = \frac{-24 \pm \sqrt{24^2 - 4 \times 18 \times 8}}{2 \times 18}$$

$$x = \frac{-24 \pm \sqrt{0}}{2 \times 18}$$

$$x = \frac{-24}{36} = -\frac{2}{3}$$

## QUESTION 31

John's weekly income consists of his hourly wages and a $50 weekly allowance given to him by his father. Maria's weekly income consists of her hourly wages and a weekly allowance given to her by her father. John earns $10 an hour and Maria earns $12 an hour. If they each work for 10 hours in one week, how much weekly allowance does Maria's father need to give her, so both Maria and John earn the same income in that week?

    A. $20

    B. $30

    C. $50

    D. $120

**Answer:** B

**Explanation:** To solve this problem, John's weekly income needs to be calculated. He earns $50 from his father and $100 from his work (10 hours × $10/hr); this adds to a total weekly income of $150. The next step is to model Maria's income as a function of her allowance and hours worked. This model is a linear equation equal to $12h + b$; where $h$ is the hours worked and $b$ is her allowance. Since the problem states Maria's income should be equal to John's income, the linear equation is set equal to $150. The problems also states she works for 10 hours, so $h$ will equal to 10 in the equation. These two substitutions result in $12 \times 10 + b = 150$, which can be solved for $b = $30.

**QUESTION 32**

Solve for x and y:

$$12x + 12y = 40$$
$$8x + 4y = 32$$

A. $x = -11\frac{1}{3}$ and $y = 14\frac{2}{3}$

B. $x = -1\frac{5}{9}$ and $y = 4\frac{8}{9}$

C. $x = 4\frac{2}{3}$ and $y = -8\frac{1}{3}$

D. $x = 4\frac{2}{3}$ and $y = -1\frac{1}{3}$

**Answer:** D

**Explanation:** The best approach is to multiply the second equation by 3. This will allow the two equations to be subtracted, and the y variable to disappear. After multiplying the second equation by 3, the equation becomes $24x + 12y = 96$. When the second equation is subtracted from the first equation, the difference is $-12x = -56$; this results in an x value of $4\frac{2}{3}$. Substituting this value for x into any of the two equations can allow solving for y. Substituting $4\frac{2}{3}$ into the first equation results in a y-value of $-1\frac{1}{3}$. The same y value will result if the x value is substituted into the second equation.

## QUESTION 33

The graph below represents the solution to which of the following inequalities

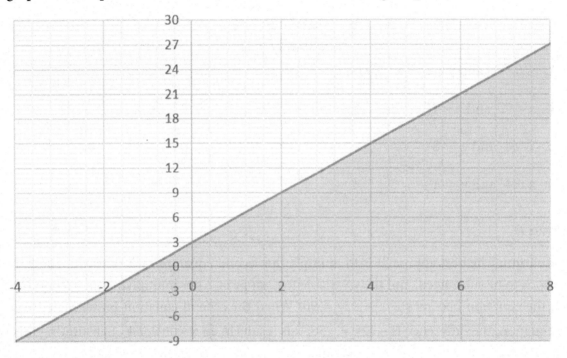

A.  y < -3x – 3

B.  y ≤ 3x + 3

C.  y < 3x + 3

D.  y ≥ 3x + 3

**Answer:** B

**Explanation:** The line indicates a linear equation defined as y= 3x + 3. The solid line indicates that values on the line are solutions to the inequality. The shading below the line indicates all values that are less than the values defined on the line are also solutions to the inequality.  These descriptions are matched with the inequality shown in answer choice B.

## QUESTION 34

What are the next three numbers in the following sequence?

10, 40, 160, 640

A. 2560, 10240, 40960

B. 10240, 40960, 163840,

C. 10, 40, 160

D. 640, 2560, 10240

**Answer:** A

**Explanation:** In the sequence, each next number is equivalent to the previous number multiplied by 4.

**QUESTION 35**

Given f(x) = 5x + 20 and g(x) = 6x + 12, what is f(g(3))?

    A.  30

    B.  35

    C.  170

    D.  222

**Answer:** C

**Explanation:** The first step is to calculate the value of g(3); this is obtained by substituting 3 for the value of x in g(x) = 6x + 12. After this substitution, g(3) = 30. Next, the value of x in f(x) = 5x + 20 must substituted with the value of g(3), which is 30. This substitution will result in 170, which is the answer.

## QUESTION 36

In his algebra class, John's professor assigns 3 group projects and 3 exams. The three group projects are worth 20%, 25%, and 20%, respectively, of the final course grade. The three exams are worth 10%, 15%, and 10% of the final course grade. If John earned a 73, 75, and 97 on the group projects, respectively, and a 99, 93, and 100 on the exams, respectively, then what is his final course grade?

A. 91.3

B. 89.5

C. 86.6

D. 78.2

**Answer:** C

**Explanation:** This problem requires the weighted average to be taken. There are 6 data values that contribute to the final course grade, and each value contributes to the final course grade differently. The 99 on the first exam has a 10% value to the final course grade, so it contributes a value of 9.9. The 93 on the second exam has a 15% value to the final course grade, so it contributes a value of 13.95. The 100 on the third exam has a 10% value to the final course grade, so it contributes a value of 10. The 73 on the first project has a value of 20% to the final course grade, so it contributes a value of 14.6. The 75 on the second project has a value of 25% to the final course grade, so it contributes a value of 18.75. The 97 on the third project has a value of 20% to the final course grade, so it contributes a value of 19.4. The 6 data values contribute a total of 9.9 + 13.95 + 10 + 14.6 + 18.75 + 19.4=86.6 to the final course grade. Since these 6 data values are the contributors to the final course grade, the final grade will be 86.6.

**QUESTION 37**

The owner of a local gym asked people in the community how many hours they work out during the week. The owner recorded his results in the line plot below. What is the median, mode, and range of the data set?

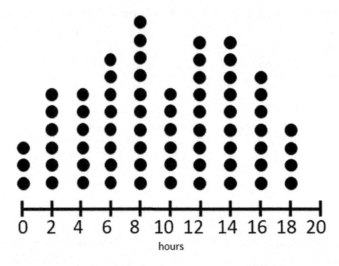

A. Median = 8; Mode = 10; Range =20

B. Median = 9; Mode = 8; Range = 18

C. Median = 10; Mode = 8; Range = 1

D. Median = 16; Mode = 10; Range = 16

**Answer:** B

**Explanation:** The mode of the data set will be 8 because 8 hours has the most values associated with it. The range of the data set will be 18 because 18 hours is the largest recorded value and 0 hours is the smallest recorded data value. The median of the data set will be 9 because the two central numbers in the data set are 8 hours and 10 hours.

# QUESTION 38

What of the following scenarios can be modeled by the line graph shown below?

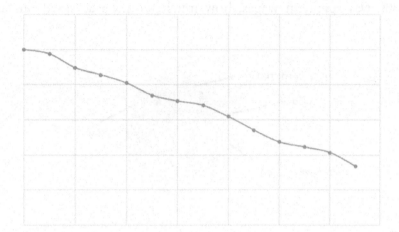

A. At the end of every year, Marcus takes his car to the dealership. The mechanic at the dealership performs the annual check-ups and tells Marcus the market value of the car. Marcus takes the value of the car at the end of each year and creates a line graph.

B. Michael takes out a loan from a bank. He pays off equal portions of the loan every month. Michael wants to create a line graph that shows the value of loan he had remaining at the end of each month that he made a payment in.

C. Maria takes out a loan from a bank. She pays off equal portions of the loan every month. Maria wants to create a line graph that shows the cumulative sum of money she has given to the bank at the end of each month.

D. A and B

**Answer:** A

**Explanation:** The line graph shown displays decreasing values of a variable with respect to increasing time. This is enough reasoning to prevent the line graph to model the situation in option C; the situation in option C has increasing values as time increases.

Furthermore, the amount of decrease with respect to time is not constant, which explains the lack of a linear relationship among the data points. Since the variable does not change constantly, option B cannot be modeled with the line graph shown. The situation in option B indicates that equal portions are paid every month, which would imply a constant change with respect to time.

Option A is the correct answer. The value of the car would decrease with respect time, and the change in the value cannot be guaranteed to be equal every year.

## QUESTION 39

The following pie chart breaks down several of the expenses for a grocery store in a given year. If a total of $923,800 was spent on wages, how much money was spent on taxes and physical capital?

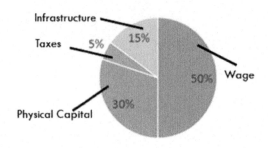

  A. $1,847,600

  B. $646,660

  C. $554,280

  D. $92,380

**Answer:** B

**Explanation:** The pie chart shows that wages take up 50% of the total expenses for the four categories. To find the total expenses for the four expense categories, the following ratio is used. The variable x represents the total expenses for the four categories.

$$\frac{1}{2} = \frac{\$923,800}{X}$$

The ratio above yields an x-value of $1,847,600. This amount of money represents the total amount of expenses for the four categories shown. The problem statement asks for the total expenses for taxes and physical capital. These two categories represent 35% of the total amount of expenses for the four categories. Thus, the total money spent on taxes and physical capital will be $1,847,600 × 0.35=$646,660.

**QUESTION 40**

Marissa's neighbors have 3 dogs. What is the probability that two of the three dogs are male?

    A.  0.875

    B.  0.500

    C.  0.375

    D.  0.250

**Answer:** D

**Explanation:** The best approach to this problem is to first list all the possible outcomes of the gender of the three dogs. This will represent the sample space. These outcomes are:

            FFF    FFM   FMF   MFF   MMM MMF  MFM  FMM

Of the sample space, only 3 of the 8 outcomes have two dogs as male, so the probably that two of the three dogs are male is 0.375.

**QUESTION 41**

Of the four options below, which data shown can be a possible probability distribution?

A.

| Y | -5 | 4 | 3 | 2 | 1 |
|------|-----|-----|-----|-----|-----|
| P(Y) | 0 | 0.1 | 0.4 | 0.3 | 0.2 |

B.

| Y | 5 | 4 | 3 | 2 | 1 |
|------|-----|-----|-----|-----|-----|
| P(Y) | 0 | 0.2 | 0.5 | 0.3 | 0.2 |

C.

| Y | A | B | C | D | E |
|------|------|-----|-----|-----|-----|
| P(Y) | -0.1 | 0.2 | 0.4 | 0.3 | 0.2 |

D.

| Y | A | B | C | D | E |
|------|-----|-----|-----|-----|-----|
| P(Y) | 0 | 0.1 | 0.4 | 0.2 | 0.2 |

**Answer:** A

**Explanation:** It is important to know the following two properties of a probability distribution:

- The probability of each event in the sample space must sum to a value of 1.00
- The probability of each event in the sample space must lie between $0 \leq P \leq 1$

Taking into account these properties, option A is chosen as the best answer.

# QUESTION 42

Find the value of:

$$\frac{5! \times 6! \times 8!}{10! \times 2! \times 0!}$$

    A. 480

    B. 690

    C. 12

    D. undefined

**Answer:** A

**Explanation:**

Method 1: Use Calculator

Method 2: Expand the Factorial(s)

If a calculator is not available, then the best approach is to expand the factorials, as shown below. (NOTE: 0! = 1)

$$\frac{(5 \times 4 \times 3 \times 2 \times 1) \times (6 \times 5 \times 4 \times 3 \times 2 \times 1) \times (8 \times 7 \times 6 \times 5 \times 4 \times 3 \times 2 \times 1)}{(10 \times 9 \times 8 \times 7 \times 6 \times 5 \times 4 \times 3 \times 2 \times 1) \times (2 \times 1) \times 1}$$

The next approach is cancel any common terms in the numerator and denominator.

$$\frac{(\cancel{5 \times 4 \times 3 \times 2 \times 1}) \times (6 \times 5 \times 4 \times 3 \times \cancel{2 \times 1}) \times (\cancel{8 \times 7} \times 6 \times 5 \times 4 \times 3 \times 2 \times \cancel{1})}{(10 \times 9 \times \cancel{8 \times 7 \times 6 \times 5 \times 4 \times 3 \times 2 \times 1}) \times (\cancel{2 \times 1}) \times \cancel{1}} = \frac{6 \times 5 \times 4 \times 3 \times 5 \times 4 \times 3 \times 2}{10 \times 9}$$

The next step is to perform the remaining operations. This results in a value of 480.

**QUESTION 43**

What is the sum of the interior angles of a nonagon?

**Answer:** 1260

**Explanation:** The interior angle of any regular polygon can be calculated with the following formula, where n represents the number of sides:

$$\frac{180 \times (n-2)}{n}$$

A nonagon has a total of 9 sides, so n will equal 9. Inputting 9 into the formula above results in a value of 140. If each angle has a measure of 140, then the total sum of the interior angles will be 1260.

**QUESTION 44**

If points ABCD are connected to form a rectangle, what is the area of this rectangle?

A. 140 feet

B. 48 feet

C. 42 feet

D. 0 feet

**Answer:** A

**Explanation:** Observation can be used to solve for the area of the rectangle. The distance from A to D is 10, and the distance A to B is 14. The area is 140 feet.

## QUESTION 45

The location of four kids playing at a park can be plotted on a Cartesian coordinate xy-plane. The first kid is at Point A. The second kid is at Point B. The third kid is at Point C. If the fourth kid is in the middle of the first and third kid, then how far is the fourth kid from the second kid?

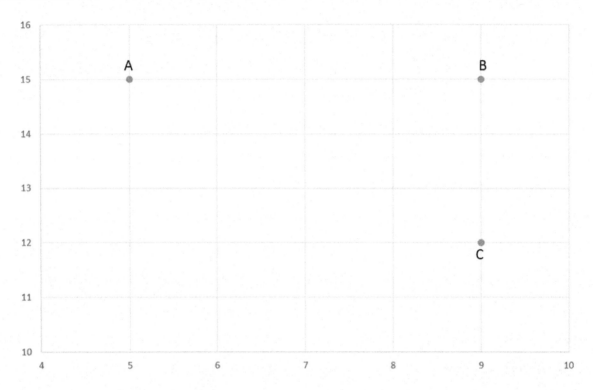

A.  2.5

B.  3

C.  4

D.  5

**Answer:** A

**Explanation:** To find the distance between the fourth kid and the second kid, the location of the fourth needs to be known.

It is known that the location of the fourth kid will be in the middle of Points A and C. This information, along with the midpoint formula, can be used to find the exact location of the fourth kid. The midpoint formula is shown below.

$$\left(\frac{x_2+x_1}{2}, \frac{y_2+y_1}{2}\right)$$

Point A has coordinate values of (5, 15). Point C has coordinate values of (9, 12). Using the coordinates of Points A and C in the midpoint formula results in a location of (7, 13.5).

With the location of the fourth kid known, the distance between the fourth kid and the second kid can be calculated with the distance formula, which is shown below.

$$d=\sqrt{(x_2-x_1)^2+(y_2-y_1)^2}$$

The fourth kid has a location of (7, 13.5). Point B has coordinate values of (9, 15). The distance between points A and B is shown below.

$$d=\sqrt{(9-7)^2+(15-13.5)^2}=2.5$$

## QUESTION 46

Which of the following reflections is done across the line y = – x?

  A.  P(x, y) --> P'(x, – y)

  B.  P(x, y) --> P'(– x, y)

  C.  P(x, y) --> P'(y, x)

  D.  P(x, y) --> P'(– y, – x)

**Answer:** D

**Explanation:** To answer the question, it is important to know the changes in the x-coordinate and y-coordinate of a point when it is reflected across the x-axis, y-axis, y = x, and y = – x.

- When a point is reflected across the x-axis, the x-coordinate remains the same and the y coordinate is multiplied by – 1.
- When a point is reflected across the y-axis, the x-coordinate is multiplied by – 1 and the y coordinate remains the same.
- When a point is reflected across the line y = x, the x-coordinate and y-coordinate change places.
- When a point is reflected across the line y = – x, the x-coordinate and y-coordinate change places and each are also multiplied by -1.

Of the options shown, only Option D shows a reflection across the line y = -x.

## QUESTION 47

Point A is located at (4, 6) and is to be shifted three units to the left and four units downward. After this translation, the point is rotated 270° about the origin. What is the location of this point after these transformations?

    A.  (2, -1)

    B.  (1, 2)

    C.  (-1, -2)

    D.  (-2, 1)

**Answer:** A

**Explanation:** A shift of three units to the left will decrease the x-coordinate value by three. For Point A, a shift three units to the left results in an x-coordinate value of 1.

A shift four units downward will decrease the y-coordinate value by four. For Point A, a shift four units downward results in a y-coordinate value of 2.

After the shifts, Point A is located at (1, 2).

A rotation of 270° causes the x coordinates and y coordinates to change places and for the y-coordinate to be multiplied by -1: P (x, y) -> P (-y, x). This effect is seen in option A.

## QUESTION 48

Which of the following histograms displays data that is right skewed?

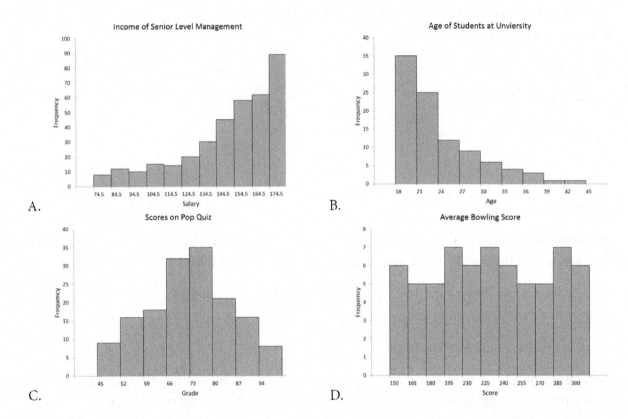

**Answer:** B

**Explanation:** Right skewed data is data in which a large number of data values are present in the lower value classes. Right skewed data will have histograms that have high peaks on the left, and peaks that gradually get smaller as the limits of the classes get large. This is seen in answer choice B.

## QUESTION 49

A principal asked the high school coach for the number of injuries students suffered in the past ten years while playing a competitive sport. Which of the following graph(s) would display the data the coach needs to give to the principal?

    A. pie graph

    B. bar graph

    C. line graph

    D. B and C

**Answer:** D

**Explanation:** A pie graph is used to compare parts of a whole. In this problem there is not enough information given to break apart the number of injuries into different groups. Furthermore, a pie graph does not show any change in the data with respect to time.

A bar graph is used to compare data belonging to different categories. In this problem there is not enough information given to break apart the number of injuries into different groups. However, the time period of ten years can be broken down into smaller years, which could represent different categories. A bar graph can be used to represent the number of injuries that occurred in the past ten years.

A line graph represents changes in a group of data over time. In this problem, the injuries represent one group of data and the time period is the ten years. A line graph can be used to represent the number of injuries that occurred in the past ten years.

## QUESTION 50

What is the solution to the following set of operations?

$$\left(\frac{5}{4}\right)^{-2} \times 5^3 \times \frac{\sqrt{18 \times 2 + 3 \times 2^2}}{80}$$

A. $4\sqrt{3}$

B. $3\sqrt{3}$

C. $3\sqrt{4}$

D. $4\sqrt{16}$

**Answer:** A

**Explanation:** To solve this problem, the order of operations needs to be considered. In this problem, there are no operations within parenthesis that need to be performed, so the only step is to evaluate the operations as they appear from left to right following the operation rules. It is important to note that a negative exponent can become positive if the term that is being raised to the negative power is inversed $(x^{-1} = (1/x)^1)$. The simplified results are:

$$\left(\frac{4}{5}\right)^2 \times 125 \times \frac{\sqrt{18 \times 2 + 3 \times 4}}{80} = \frac{16}{25} \times 125 \times \frac{\sqrt{36 + 12}}{80} = \sqrt{48} = \sqrt{16 \times 3} = 4\sqrt{3}$$

## QUESTION 51

Which of the following is NOT equivalent to the radical below?

$$\sqrt[3]{324}$$

A. $3 \times \sqrt[3]{12}$

B. $\left(\dfrac{1}{324}\right)^{\frac{1}{3}}$

C. $\left((324)^2\right)^{\frac{1}{6}}$

D. 18

**Answer:** D

**Explanation:** The best approach to this problem is to evaluate each option choice given and to see whether or not it equals the expression given.

To determine if the first option is equivalent to the expression given, it is necessary to input $3^3$ into the radical $\sqrt[3]{12}$. This results in $\sqrt[3]{12 \times 27} = \sqrt[3]{324}$, which is equivalent to the expression given.

Option B is equivalent to the expression given. It is just expressed in a different format.

To determine if the third option is equivalent to the expression given, it is necessary to multiply the two exponent, which results in an exponent of 1/3. The originally expression had 324 raised to an exponent of 1/3, so this option is equivalent to the expression given.

If a calculator is used to evaluate the original expression, it would result in a value of 6.87 not 18. Thus, the third option is incorrect.

## QUESTION 52

Which of the following options is not true?

 A. Examples of real numbers are: $0.7458, \frac{1}{2}, -4.254, 0, 1, 5.254, -\sqrt{2.254}$

 B. Examples of whole numbers are: $0, 2, \frac{4}{2}, \sqrt{25}, 100$

 C. Example of irrational numbers: $\sqrt{23}, \pi, \sqrt{2}, \sqrt{-25}$

 D. Examples of natural numbers: $1, 2, 3, 28, 45897$

**Answer:** C

**Explanation:** $\sqrt{-25} = \sqrt{25}\sqrt{-1} = 5i$, which is an imaginary number.

## QUESTION 53

For a charity event, a basket was passed around, and people were asked to place any amount of money they desired into the basket. Jerry was the first person to receive the basket and he put in $100. Jacob was the next person and he decided to place 26% of what he saw in the basket. Timmy was the third recipient of the basket and he decided to place 125% of what he saw in the basket. Maria received the basket next and she placed $20 into the basket. Bob received the basket next and he placed 0.05% of what he saw in the basket. Bob's wife saw the basket next, and she placed 150% of what she in the basket. How much money has accumulated in the basket so far?

- A. $421.02

- B. $630.75

- C. $759.13

- D. $796.69

**Answer:** C

**Explanation:** The best approach is to evaluate the amount of money in the basket after each person has placed money in it.

After Jerry placed $100 into the basket, there was a total of $100 in the basket.

Jacob placed 26% of the $100 in the basket. 26% of $100 is $26. After Jacob placed this amount of money in the basket, there was a total of $126 in the basket.

Timmy placed 125% of $126. This calculated to be a donation of $\frac{125}{100} \times \$126 = \$157.50$. After this donation, there was a total of $283.50 in the basket.

Maria added $20 to the basket to increase the total donation to $283.50 + 20 = \$303.50$.

Bob placed 0.05% of $303.50. This calculated to be a donation of $\frac{0.05}{100} \times \$303.50 = \$0.15$. After this donation, there was a total of $303.65 in the basket.

Bob's wife placed 150% of $303.65. This calculates to be a donation of $\frac{150}{100} \times \$303.65 = 455.48\$$. After this donation, there was a total of $759.13 in the basket.

Since Bob's wife is the last person to put money into the basket, the current amount of money accumulated is $759.13.

## QUESTION 54

At an athletic department store, the ratio of basketball jerseys to baseball jerseys is 8 to 3, and the ratio of football jerseys to soccer jerseys is 1 to 5. If the ratio of baseball jerseys to soccer jerseys is 7 to 4 and there are a total of 350 basketball jerseys, then how many football jerseys are at the store?

    A.  15

    B.  375

    C.  2000

    D.  350

**Answer:** A

**Explanation:** The first approach is to determine the ratio of basketball jerseys to football jerseys. The best approach is to write the ratios in fraction form; this is shown below:

$$\frac{\text{basketball}}{\text{baseball}} = \frac{8}{3}, \frac{\text{football}}{\text{soccer}} = \frac{1}{5}, \frac{\text{baseball}}{\text{soccer}} = \frac{7}{4}$$

To find the ratio of basketball jerseys to the football jerseys, the ratio of basketball jerseys to baseball jerseys needs to be multiplied by the ratio of baseball jerseys to soccer jerseys. Then, the result needs to be multiplied by the inverse of the ratio of football jerseys to soccer jerseys. These operations are summarized below:

$$\frac{\text{basketball}}{\text{baseball}} \times \frac{\text{baseball}}{\text{soccer}} \times \frac{\text{soccer}}{\text{football}}$$

$$\frac{8}{3} \times \frac{7}{4} \times \frac{5}{1} = \frac{70}{3}$$

The result of the operations shows that the ratio of basketball jerseys to football jerseys is $\frac{70}{3}$.

The ratio analysis above has shown that the ratio of basketball jerseys to football jerseys is $\frac{70}{3}$. Since it is known that there is a total of 350 basketball jerseys, the following proportion can be developed. After solving this proportion, x, which is the number of football jerseys, is calculated to be 15.

$$\frac{\text{basketball}}{\text{football}} = \frac{350}{x} = \frac{70}{3}$$

$$1050 = 70x$$

$$x = 15$$

**QUESTION 55**

Which of the following answer choices contains a prime number, a composite number, an odd number, an even number, a factor of 126, a multiple of 7, and a number divisible by 36? Furthermore, the answer choice should contain 7 unique numbers and be arranged in order from least to greatest.

    A. {3, 9, 13, 16, 21, 35, 72}

    B. {1, 6, 7, 13, 21, 35, 108}

    C. {11, 15, 13, 18, 32, 49, 36}

    D. {13, 25, 30, 252, 700, 3600}

**Answer:** A

**Explanation:** To answer this problem, the following definitions need to be known:

- Prime Number: a natural number that can only be divided by one and itself; one is not a prime number
- Composite Number: a number that is a product of two or more prime numbers
- Odd Number: numbers that are not multiple of 2
- Even Number: all numbers that are multiple of 2, including zero
- Factor: a component of a multiplication
- Multiple: the results of a number being multiplied by each natural number
- Divisible: when a number divides another number evenly

With these definitions known, it is best to go through each option choice and evaluate whether it satisfies the required constraints: A quick glance at option A shows that there are 7 numbers and they are arranged from least to greatest. The number 3 satisfied the prime number requirement. The number 9 satisfies the composite number requirement (factors: 1, 3, and 9). The number 13 satisfies the odd number requirement. The number 16 satisfies the even number requirement. The number 21 satisfies the requirement of having a number that is a factor of 21×6=126. The number 35 satisfies the requirement of having a multiple of 7×5=35. The number 72 satisfies the requirement of having a number divisible by 72/36=2. Since all the numbers in this option satisfy the requirements, Option A is correct.

This page is intentionally left blank.

# Practice Test 2

This page is intentionally left blank.

## Exam Answer Sheet – Test 2

Below is an optional answer sheet to use to document answers.

| Question Number | Selected Answer | Question Number | Selected Answer |
|---|---|---|---|
| 1 | | 31 | |
| 2 | | 32 | |
| 3 | | 33 | |
| 4 | | 34 | |
| 5 | | 35 | |
| 6 | | 36 | |
| 7 | | 37 | |
| 8 | | 38 | |
| 9 | | 39 | |
| 10 | | 40 | |
| 11 | | 41 | |
| 12 | | 42 | |
| 13 | | 43 | |
| 14 | | 44 | |
| 15 | | 45 | |
| 16 | | 46 | |
| 17 | | 47 | |
| 18 | | 48 | |
| 19 | | 49 | |
| 20 | | 50 | |
| 21 | | 51 | |
| 22 | | 52 | |
| 23 | | 53 | |
| 24 | | 54 | |
| 25 | | 55 | |
| 26 | | | |
| 27 | | | |
| 28 | | | |
| 29 | | | |
| 30 | | | |

This page is intentionally left blank.

**QUESTION 1**

Which of the following is equivalent to $2^x + 12^x$?

    A. $14^x$

    B. $24^x$

    C. $2^x(1 + 6^x)$

    D. $3 \times 4^x$

**Answer:**

**QUESTION 2**

Every month, a telephone company charges $0.10 for each minute of telephone usage in that month. If a customer exceeds the limit of 700 minutes per month, then for every additional minute, the charge per minute increases to $0.15. Which expression below is equal to the monthly telephone usage charge, expressed as variable c, for a customer who used the telephone for 24 hours in one month?

    A. $c = 700 \times \$0.15 + 740 \times \$0.10$

    B. $c = 1440 \times \$0.15$

    C. $c = 1440 \times \$0.10$

    D. $c = 700 \times 0.10 + 740 \times \$0.15$

**Answer:**

**QUESTION 3**

In Edward's class, there are 12 boys for every 20 girls. What percent of the total class are girls?

    A. 62.5%

    B. 60%

    C. 80%

    D. 85%

**Answer:**

## QUESTION 4

What equation represents the graph shown below?

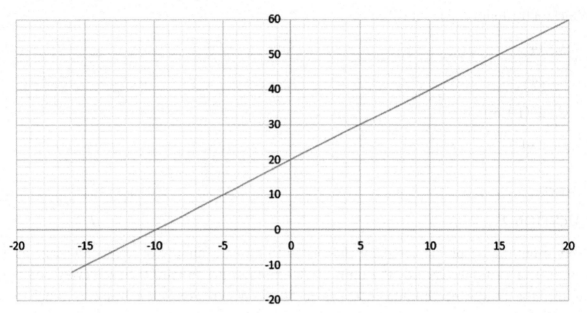

A.  y = x + 20

B.  y = -2x

C.  y = 2x + 20

D.  y = 2x - 20

**Answer:**

## QUESTION 5

Which of the following equations will NOT produce the graph shown below?

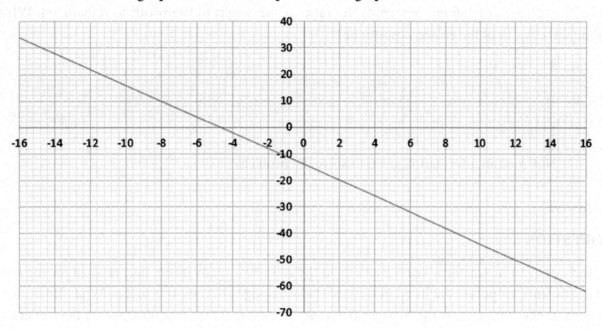

A.  $y = -3x - 14$

B.  $y = - (3x + 14)$

C.  $y - 4 = -3 (x + 6)$

D.  $y - 20 = -3 (x + 2)$

**Answer:**

## QUESTION 6

Solve the following:

$$1 + 5 \times \left(\frac{1}{3}\right)^{-1} \times 6 + 2 \times 3$$

**Answer:**

## QUESTION 7

Joanna wants to enlarge the rectangular poster on her wall. She wants to enlarge the poster so it can have an area of 256 in², but wants the ratio of the height to the width to remain 1:4. What should the width of the enlarged poster be?

A.  8

B.  16

C.  32

D.  Not enough information given to solve the problem

**Answer:**

## QUESTION 8

After a test, an instructor asked 5 students in the class how many hours they studied for the test. The students' responses are listed in the table below along with their test scores. What function, if any, describes the relationship between the hours studied and the score obtained by the students?

| Student | Hours Studied | Exam Score |
|---|---|---|
| 1 | 15 | 70 |
| 2 | 20 | 80 |
| 3 | 3 | 46 |
| 4 | 1 | 42 |
| 5 | 30 | 100 |

A.  $e(h) = h^2 - 120$

B.  $e(h) = 3h + 20$

C.  $e(h) = 2h + 40$

D.  None of the above

**Answer:**

104

## QUESTION 9

If Y is the dependent variable in the tables below, which of the following tables contains values that does not defines a function?

A

| X | Y |
|---|---|
| 5 | 123 |
| 8 | 510 |
| 12 | 1726 |
| 18 | 5830 |
| 23 | 12165 |

B

| X | Y |
|---|---|
| -10 | 15 |
| -5 | 10 |
| 0 | 5 |
| 5 | 10 |
| 10 | 15 |

C

| X | Y |
|---|---|
| -10 | 913 |
| -8 | 457 |
| 0 | -7 |
| 16 | -4391 |
| 24 | -14455 |

D

| X | Y |
|---|---|
| 12 | 114 |
| 20 | 210 |
| 30 | 330 |
| 37 | 414 |
| 37 | 444 |

**Answer:**

## QUESTION 10

What value(s) of x are NOT included in the domain of this function?

$$f(x) = \frac{x^2 + 5x - 14}{x^2 - 7x + 10}$$

A.  x = −2, x = −5

B.  x = 7

C.  x = −5

D.  x = 2, x = 5, and x = −7

**Answer:**

## QUESTION 11

A cable connects the top of a post with the ground as shown in the figure below. The distance between the base of the tower and the base of the cable is 36 feet, and the cable has an angle of elevation of 35° with respect to the ground.

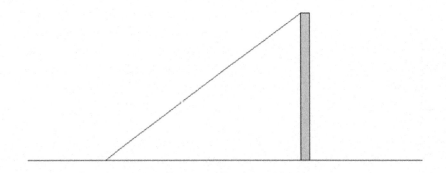

Note: Figure not drawn to scale.

What is the approximate height in feet of the post?

A.  17

B.  20

C.  22

D.  25

**Answer:**

**QUESTION 12**

Which of the following functions cannot be classified as an even function?

    A.  $|x| + 3 = f(x)$

    B.  $x^2 + 3 = f(x)$

    C.  $x^4 + 3 = f(x)$

    D.  $x + 3 = f(x)$

**Answer:**

**QUESTION 13**

Given that points I, J, and K represent the midpoints for their respective sides on △ABC, what is the perimeter of triangle ABC?

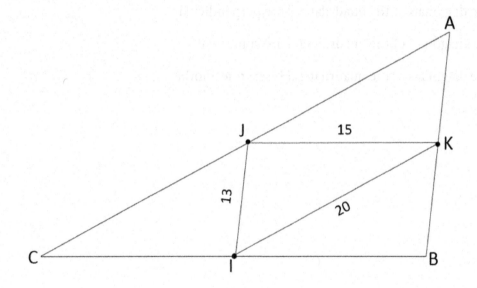

    A.  48

    B.  72

    C.  96

    D.  108

**Answer:**

## QUESTION 14

In parallelogram ABCD (not shown), ∢B = x + 15 and ∢C = 3x + 5. Which of the following statements regarding the diagonals of the parallelogram is true?

    A. $\overline{BD} = \overline{CA}$

    B. $\overline{BD} < \overline{CA}$

    C. $\overline{BD} > \overline{CA}$

    D. Not enough information given

**Answer:**

## QUESTION 15

Which of the following statements accurately describes a rhombus?

    A. The diagonals of the quadrilateral are perpendicular

    B. The diagonals of the quadrilateral are congruent

    C. The diagonals of the quadrilateral bisect one another

    D. A and C

**Answer:**

# QUESTION 16

Which of the following line segment(s) represents a chord on the circle shown below?

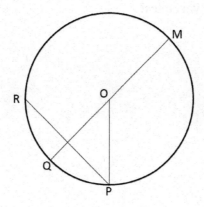

A. $\overline{RP}$

B. $\overline{PO}$

C. $\overline{MQ}$

D. A and C

**Answer:**

## QUESTION 17

Which of the following scatter plots shows that there may be some degree of correlation between the dependent and independent variables?

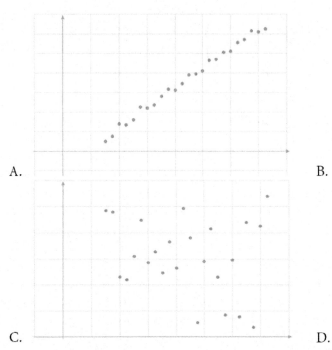

A.

C.

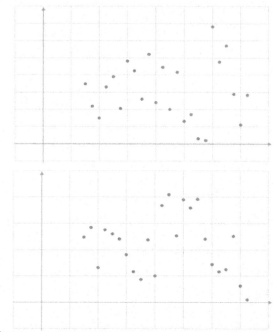

B.

D.

**Answer:**

## QUESTION 18

When a six sided standard die is tossed once, what is the probability of getting 1, 3, and a 9?

    A. $\frac{1}{6}$

    B. $\frac{3}{6}$

    C. 0

    D. Undefined

**Answer:**

**QUESTION 19**

Sets A and B are defined below. Which of the following sets represents A∩ B?

$$A = \{3, 6, 9, 12, 15, 18\}$$

$$B = \{2, 4, 6, 8, 10, 12, 14\}$$

A. {2, 3, 4, 6, 8, 9, 10, 12, 14, 15, 18}

B. 2, 3, 4, 6, 8, 9, 10, 12, 14, 15, 18

C. {6, 12}

D. A and B

**Answer:**

**QUESTION 20**

A set has the following 10 numbers: 12, 19, 25, 28, 54, 26, 87, 23, 98, and 25. If an $11^{th}$ number is to be added to the set, what does the number have to be in order for the set to have a mean of 40?

A. -43

B. 3

C. 40

D. 43

**Answer:**

## QUESTION 21

A data set with a mean of 75 and a standard deviation of 3.5 is known to have a normal distribution. What percent of the data does NOT lie between 71.5 and 78.5?

    A. 99.95

    B. 68.2

    C. 31.8

    D. not enough information given

**Answer:**

## QUESTION 22

Which of the following ratios is not equal to 68%?

    A. 68:100

    B. 34:50

    C. 102:150

    D. 17:50

**Answer:**

## QUESTION 23

Solve the following problem:

$$(5-1\times0+3\div3)\times(5+3\times2^4)\times\left(\frac{21\times3\times\frac{1}{7}}{5-1\times4\times3+2}\right)$$

    A. 0

    B. -572.4

    C. -230.4

    D. 57.24

**Answer:**

**QUESTION 24**

Chris' family drove a distance of 300 miles in 2 hours. Pat's family drove a distance of 400 miles in 3 hours. What is the ratio of the speed of Chris' family to the speed of Pat's family?

    A. 9/8

    B. 8/9

    C. 3/4

    D. 2/3

**Answer:**

**QUESTION 25**

Which of the following represents the Commutative Property of Multiplication?

    A. $a \times b \times c = a \times b^c$

    B. $a \times b \times c = b \times c \times a$

    C. $a \times b \times c = a \times b \times c$

    D. $a \times b \times c = a + b + c$

**Answer:**

## QUESTION 26

What are the values for the domain in the graph shown below?

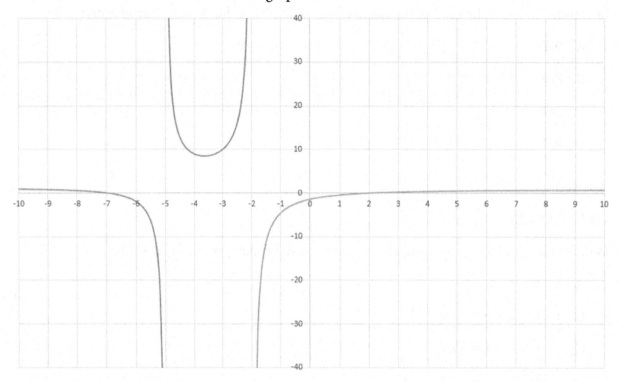

A. $[-5, -2]$

B. $[-\infty, -5) \cup (-5, -2) \cup (-2, \infty]$

C. $(-\infty, -5) \cup [-5, -2] \cup (-2, \infty)$

D. None of the above

**Answer:**

**QUESTION 27**

If the sum of two consecutive integers is 125, then what are the integers?

60, 61, 62, 63, 64

**Answer:**

**QUESTION 28**

Of the following equations, which equation has an x – intercept greater than the y – intercept and a slope equal to the absolute value of the y – intercept.

A.  y = 2x – 2

B.  y = 4x – 16

C.  y = 0.5x – 0.5

D.  A and C

**Answer:**

**QUESTION 29**

What would be the y-intercept of the graph?

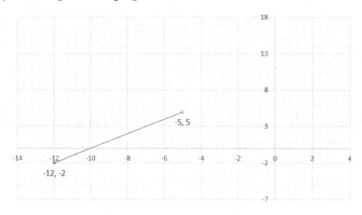

    A.  13

    B.  10

    C.  -14

    D.  -10

**Answer:**

**QUESTION 30**

The table below shows the length of time in minutes 25 drivers were stuck in traffic during rush hour. Which of the following values cannot be determined from the data set shown below?

| Time | Number of Drivers |
|---|---|
| 0.0-5.5 | 3 |
| 5.5-15.5 | 10 |
| 15.5-25.5 | 8 |
| 25.5-30.5 | 1 |
| 30.5-45.5 | 3 |

    A.  range

    B.  mean

    C.  median

    D.  cannot be answered

**Answer:**

# QUESTION 31

A new ice cream store has opened, and the owner of the store has surveyed the first 100 customers. The survey showed that 67 customers have tried their homemade chocolate flavor and 82 customers have tried their homemade vanilla flavor. Of the 100 customers surveyed, 27 customers have tried the homemade vanilla flavor but not the homemade chocolate flavor. How many customers have tried neither the homemade vanilla flavor nor the homemade chocolate flavor?

   A. 6

   B. 12

   C. 40

   D. 55

**Answer:**

# QUESTION 32

Mark and his wife are at the grand opening of a car dealership because they each want to win the two prizes that are being raffled away. Every attendee at the grand opening is allowed to write one name on a slip of paper and place that paper into a jar. Each attendee can get one prize. The manager will then select one name from the jar, and this person will have the option of choosing his or her prize. The manger will then select another name from the jar, and this person will take the remaining prize. If Mark and his wife have counted a total of 320 slips in the jar, what is the probability that they will each go home with a prize.

   A. $9.80 \times 10^{-6}$

   B. $6.25 \times 10^{-3}$

   C. $9.77 \times 10^{-6}$

   D. $1.96 \times 10^{-5}$

**Answer:**

**QUESTION 33**

Which of the following events are mutually exclusive?

A. The event of a getting an odd number and an even number when a single card is drawn from a deck.

B. The event of getting a 3 and an odd number when a die is tossed.

C. The event of getting 7 and a number less than 9 when a single card is drawn from a deck.

D. The event of getting a 5 and a number less than 6 when a die is tossed.

**Answer:**

**QUESTION 34**

On a school field trip, Timothy has to choose a walking buddy to accompany him to the vending machine. Of the thirty students he can choose from, 20 are older than him and 10 are younger than him. Of the 20 students older than Timothy, 12 are boys, and of the 10 students younger than him, 6 are girls. What is the probability that Timothy chooses a walking buddy that is older than him or a boy?

A. $\frac{6}{5}$

B. $\frac{2}{3}$

C. $\frac{4}{5}$

D. $\frac{11}{15}$

**Answer:**

**QUESTION 35**

Which of the following situations describes dependent events?

    A.  The probability of selecting a quarter from a piggy bank and then selecting a penny.

    B.  The probability of getting 3 from a single toss of a die and then another 3 from another toss of the die.

    C.  The probability of selecting a quarter from a piggy bank and then selecting a penny after the quarter has been put back.

    D.  A and C

**Answer:**

**QUESTION 36**

A shoe store receives a weekly shipment of 100 shoes on Sunday night, so that it can have full inventory to sell from on Monday morning. In a certain week, the store manager was notified that the shipment for that week contained 5 shoes that were damaged due to mishandling. If this notification came Tuesday, and 5 of the 100 delivered shoes were sold the previous day (Monday), what is the probability that at least 1 of the 5 shoes sold was damaged?

    A.  0.05

    B.  0.230

    C.  0.770

    D.  0.95

**Answer:**

## QUESTION 37

Coach Johnson tells his quarterback to stand 50 yards away from the poster shown below, and throw the football at the shaded circle. The intention of this drill is to improve the accuracy of the quarterback's throws. If the quarterback's throw hits the poster, what is the probability that it will hit the shaded circle?

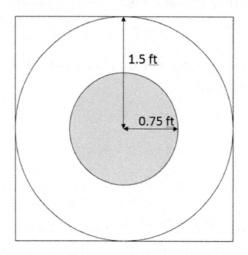

A. 0.196

B. 0.250

C. 0.520

D. 0.785

**Answer:**

## QUESTION 38

Of the equations below, which equation does NOT have an x–intercept of 5 and a y–intercept of 15?

    A. $y = -3x + 15$

    B. $y + 15 = -2 \times (x - 15)$

    C. $2y = -6x + 30$

    D. $y - 9 = -3 \times (x - 2)$

**Answer:**

## QUESTION 39

Which of the following line(s) represents an axis of symmetry for $y = 6x^2 + 24x - 24$?

    A. $x = -2$

    B. $x = -2$ and $y = -24$

    C. $x = 2$

    D. $x = 0$

**Answer:**

## QUESTION 40

Which of the following expressions is equivalent to the expression below?

$$\left(\frac{6-x}{5x-30}\right)^{-1} \times \left(\frac{5yx+5y}{10yx+5yx}\right)$$

    A. $\dfrac{(x+1)}{15x}$

    B. $\dfrac{-5y(x+6)}{3x}$

    C. $\dfrac{-5(x+1)}{3x}$

    D. $\dfrac{3(x+1)}{5}$

**Answer:**

**QUESTION 41**

If the following equation was altered such that b was preceded by a negative sign, h was reduced by −3, and k was increased by 4, then how would the graph of the equation be altered?

$$y = b (x - h)^2 + k$$

A. The graph will shift three units to the left, shift upwards 4 units, and invert.

B. The graph will shift three units to the right and shift upwards 4 units.

C. The graph will shift three units to the right, shift upwards 4 units, and invert.

D. The graph will shift three units to the right, shift downwards 4 units, and invert.

**Answer:**

**QUESTION 42**

Jimmy has obtained a summer job that will last 10 weeks. Jimmy will receive $13 an hour, and will also receive a $200 signing bonus during his first week. If Jimmy plans to work 40 hours each week, which graph shows the cumulative sum of his income throughout the 10 week period?

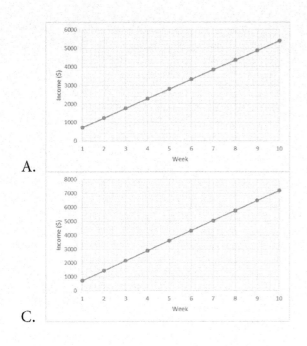

A.

B.

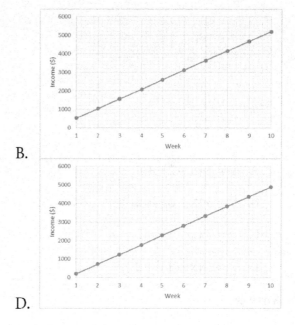

C.

D.

**Answer:**

## QUESTION 43

If the following curve it shifted three units to the left and two units down, what will be the new equation representing the graph?

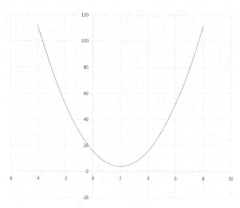

A.  $y = 3(x - 2)^2 + 4$

B.  $y = 3(x - 5)^2 + 2$

C.  $y = 3(x - 3)^2 - 2$

D.  $y = 3(x + 1)^2 + 2$

**Answer:**

What function is represented by the graph below?

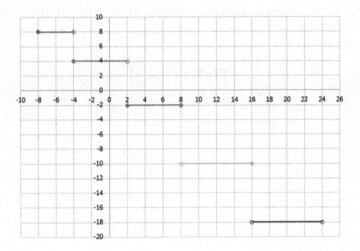

A. $\left\{\begin{array}{l} 8;\ -8\leq x<-4 \\ 4;\ -4\leq x<2 \\ -2;\ 2\leq x\leq8 \\ -10;\ 8<x\leq16 \\ -18;16<x<24 \end{array}\right\}$

B. $\left\{\begin{array}{l} 8;\ -8<x<-2 \\ 4;\ -4<x<2 \\ -2;\ 2<x<8 \\ -10;\ 8<x<16 \\ -18;16<x<24 \end{array}\right\}$

C. $\left\{\begin{array}{l} 8;\ -8\leq x\leq-2 \\ 4;\ -4\leq x\leq2 \\ -2;\ 2\leq x\leq8 \\ -10;\ 8\leq x\leq16 \\ -18;16\leq x\leq24 \end{array}\right\}$

D. $\left\{\begin{array}{l} 8;\ -8<x\leq-2 \\ 4;\ -4<x\leq2 \\ -2;\ 2<x<8 \\ -10;\ 8\leq x<16 \\ -18;16\leq x\leq24 \end{array}\right\}$

**Answer:**

**QUESTION 45**

The following equation can be used to convert between degrees Fahrenheit and degrees Celsius. If it was reported to be 30 degrees Celsius outside, then what is the temperature in degrees Fahrenheit?

$$F° = 32 + \left( °C + \frac{9}{5} \right)$$

A. 51°

B. 83°

C. 86°

D. 123.8°

**Answer:**

**QUESTION 46**

If a = 2, b = 3, c = 1, and d = 4, then the expression below is equivalent to what numerical value?

$$a \times (b + c \times a) - b \times c + \frac{d \times d \times a}{c}$$

A. 18

B. 35

C. 39

D. 43

**Answer:**

**QUESTION 47**

In the figure below, point P bisects line segment $\overline{LN}$. Point O bisects line segment $\overline{LP}$. Point Q bisects line segment $\overline{PN}$. If it is known that line segment $\overline{MP}$ is perpendicular to line segment $\overline{LN}$, then which of the following statements regarding the area of the triangles is true.

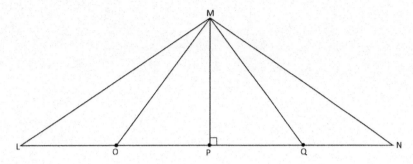

   A.  ΔMOP = ΔMPN

   B.  ΔMLO = ΔMPN

   C.  ΔMOP = ΔMQP = ΔMLO = ΔMNQ

   D.  ΔMOP > ΔMLO

**Answer:**

**QUESTION 48**

Which of the following shapes may NOT be similar?

   A.  a pair of two isosceles triangles

   B.  a pair of two squares

   C.  a pair of two regular hexagons

   D.  a pair of two regular octagons

**Answer:**

**QUESTION 49**

A 50ft building casts a shadow that extends a lateral length of 75ft. If a similar building of 150ft tall is in the same area, how far will the shadow extend?

   A. 90.1ft

   B. 150ft

   C. 225ft

   D. 270.5ft

**Answer:**

**QUESTION 50**

Which of the following statements defines the conditions necessary for shapes to be similar?

   A. all pairs of corresponding angles are congruent

   B. all pairs of corresponding sides are proportional

   C. all pairs of corresponding angles and sides are congruent

   D. A and B

**Answer:**

**QUESTION 51**

A soda can has a total surface area of $35\pi$ in². If the height of the right circular cylinder is 2 inches greater than the radius of the circular base, what is the length of the diameter of the circular base?

   A. 10.0 inches

   B. 8.4 inches

   C. 6.6 inches

   D. 5.0 inches

**Answer:**

## QUESTION 52

An ice cream store owner purchases ice cream from a vendor in 5 gallon buckets. He sells this ice cream in cones to his customers. When selling the ice cream, the owner fills the cone with ice cream and adds an extra scoop of the ice cream on the top. Each cone has a height of 7 inches and a circular base of diameter 4 inches. The extra scoop of ice cream is in the shape of a hemisphere with a radius 2 inches. If the owner purchases cones in packages of 10, how many packages are needed for every bucket of ice cream bought? (Assume the cone has the shape of a right circular cone. Also, 7.48 gal = 1 ft³)

A. 1 package

B. 2 packages

C. 3 packages

D. 4 packages

**Answer:**

## QUESTION 53

Which of the following properties regarding circles is not true?

A. A line tangent to the circle only touches the circle at one point.

B. A line secant to the circle joints two points on the circumference.

C. A central angle of a circle is an angle in which the vertex lies at the center of the circle and its sides are radii of the circle.

D. Concentric circles must be congruent to one another.

**Answer:**

## QUESTION 54

What is the distance between points (3, -9) and (4, 8)?

**Answer:**

**QUESTION 55**

The governor of a Ohio was given a report of the number of parks in each county within the state. After looking at the report, the governor became curious about certain data points. If the following numbers were in the report, which numbers most likely caught the governor's attention?

| County | 1 | 2 | 3 | 4 | 5 | 6 | 7 | 8 | 9 | 10 | 11 | 12 | 13 | 14 | 15 | 16 | 17 | 18 | 19 | 20 |
|---|---|---|---|---|---|---|---|---|---|---|---|---|---|---|---|---|---|---|---|---|
| Number of Parks | 7 | 8 | 6 | 5 | 9 | 5 | 5 | 5 | 6 | 6 | 7 | 1 | 0 | 15 | 8 | 8 | 6 | 5 | 6 | 7 |

    A.  County 12, 13, 14

    B.  County 13

    C.  County 14

    D.  County 4, 6, 7, 8, and 18

**Answer:**

# Middle School Practice Exam Answers – Test 2

| Question Number | Selected Answer | Question Number | Selected Answer |
|---|---|---|---|
| 1 | C | 31 | A |
| 2 | D | 32 | D |
| 3 | A | 33 | A |
| 4 | C | 34 | C |
| 5 | D | 35 | A |
| 6 | 97 | 36 | B |
| 7 | C | 37 | A |
| 8 | C | 38 | B |
| 9 | D | 39 | A |
| 10 | A | 40 | C |
| 11 | D | 41 | C |
| 12 | D | 42 | A |
| 13 | C | 43 | D |
| 14 | C | 44 | A |
| 15 | D | 45 | C |
| 16 | D | 46 | C |
| 17 | A | 47 | C |
| 18 | C | 48 | A |
| 19 | C | 49 | C |
| 20 | D | 50 | D |
| 21 | C | 51 | D |
| 22 | D | 52 | C |
| 23 | B | 53 | D |
| 24 | A | 54 | 17.03 |
| 25 | B | 55 | D |
| 26 | D | | |
| 27 | 62, 63 | | |
| 28 | D | | |
| 29 | B | | |
| 30 | D | | |

NOTE: Getting approximately 80% of the questions correct increases chances of obtaining passing score on the real exam. This varies from different states and university programs.

This page is intentionally left blank.

## QUESTION 1

Which of the following is equivalent to $2^x + 12^x$?

    A. $14^x$

    B. $24^x$

    C. $2^x(1 + 6^x)$

    D. $3 \times 4^x$

**Answer:** C

**Explanation:** It is important to note that $12^x = (2 \times 6)^x = 2^x \times 6^x$. With this equivalency, an expression of $2^x + 2^x \times 6^x$ can be factored. The common factor in both terms of the addition is $2^x$. When this factor is taken out of the expression the result is $2^x(1 + 6^x)$.

## QUESTION 2

Every month, a telephone company charges $0.10 for each minute of telephone usage in that month. If a customer exceeds the limit of 700 minutes per month, then for every additional minute, the charge per minute increases to $0.15. Which expression below is equal to the monthly telephone usage charge, expressed as variable c, for a customer who used the telephone for 24 hours in one month?

    A.  $c = 700 \times \$0.15 + 740 \times \$0.10$

    B.  $c = 1440 \times \$0.15$

    C.  $c = 1440 \times \$0.10$

    D.  $c = 700 \times 0.10 + 740 \times \$0.15$

**Answer:** D

**Explanation:** The telephone usage charge can consists of two separate expenditures. The first expenditure will be the cost for using the telephone for up to 700 minutes. The second expenditure, which may or may not exist, is for using the telephone for any minutes in excess of 700 minutes. In this problem, it is stated that the total usage is 24 hours, which is equivalent to $24 \times 60 = 1440$ minutes. Since 1440 minutes is greater than 700 minutes, the second expenditure will exist. The first expenditure will be the cost of the first 700 minutes used, which can be expressed by $700 \times \$0.10$. The second expenditure will be for the cost of the 740 minutes in excess of the $1440 - 700 = 740$ minutes, which can be expressed as $740 \times \$0.15$. The total cost is the sum of the two expenditures and is expressed by answer choice D.

**QUESTION 3**

In Edward's class, there are 12 boys for every 20 girls. What percent of the total class are girls?

    A.  62.5%

    B.  60%

    C.  80%

    D.  85%

**Answer:** A

**Explanation:** If there are 12 boys for every 20 girls in the class, then, for a total of 32 students, there will be 20 girls. 20 girls for every 32 students represents a percentage of $\left(\frac{20}{32}\right) \times 100\% =$ 62.5%.

## QUESTION 4

What equation represents the graph shown below?

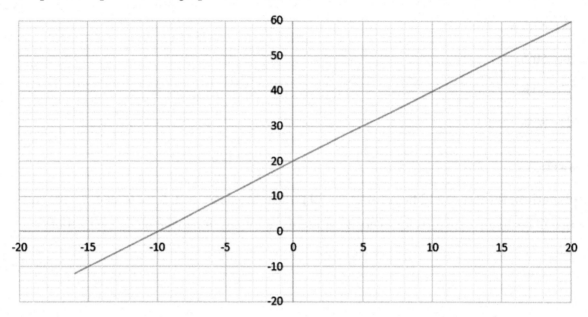

A. y = x + 20

B. y = -2x

C. y = 2x + 20

D. y = 2x - 20

**Answer:** C

**Explanation:** Each of the answer choices given above are in the standard form of a linear equation: y = mx + b; where m is the slope and b is the y-intercept. The graph shown above has a y-intercept of 20. The slope can be calculated by choosing two points and using the slope formula, which is shown below. The two points chosen can be (0, 20) and (10, 40); these two points result in a slope of 2. Thus, the linear equation is: y = 2x + 20.

$$m = \frac{y_2 - y_1}{x_2 - x_1}$$

$$m = \frac{40-20}{10-0} = 2$$

**QUESTION 5**

Which of the following equations will NOT produce the graph shown below?

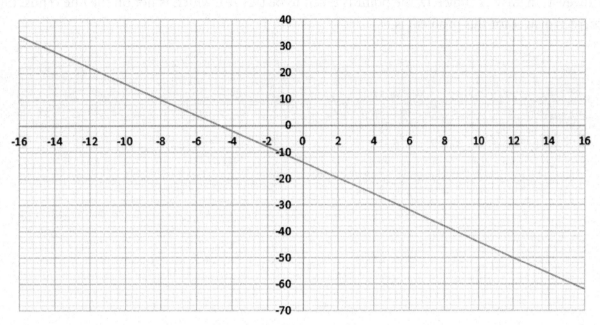

A. $y = -3x - 14$

B. $y = -(3x + 14)$

C. $y - 4 = -3(x + 6)$

D. $y - 20 = -3(x + 2)$

**Answer:** D

**Explanation:** The answer choices are the linear equations in two different formats: the point-slope formula and the standard formula.

The standard formula is expressed as $y = mx + b$; where m is the slope and b is the y intercept. In this graph, the y – intercept can be read as -14. The slope can be calculated from the slope formula, which is shown below. Two points are necessary to calculate the slope; these two points are chosen to be (2, -20) and (4, -26). The points result in a slope of -3. Thus, the equation of the graph in standard linear form is $y = -3x - 14$. This is also equivalent to $y = -(3x + 14)$.

$$m = \frac{y_2 - y_1}{x_2 - x_1}$$

$$m = \frac{-26 - (-20)}{4 - 2} = -3$$

The point slope formula is expressed as $y - y_1 = m(x - x_1)$; where m is the slope and $(x_1, y_1)$ is a point on the line. In answer choice C, the point is taken to be (-6, 4), which is a point on the line. However, in answer choice D, the point is taken to be (-2, 20), which is not on the line. Thus, the correct answer for this problem is D.

## QUESTION 6

Solve the following:

$$1 + 5 \times \left(\frac{1}{3}\right)^{-1} \times 6 + 2 \times 3$$

**Answer:** 97

**Explanation:** The answer to this problem will come from performing the operations in the proper order.

The first step is to evaluate $\left(\frac{1}{3}\right)^{-1}$, which is equivalent to 3.

The next step is to evaluate $5 \times 3 \times 6$, which is equivalent to 90.

The next step is to evaluate $2 \times 3$, which is equivalent to 6.

The final step is to evaluate $1 + 90 + 6$, which results in the final answer of 97.

## QUESTION 7

Joanna wants to enlarge the rectangular poster on her wall. She wants to enlarge the poster so it can have an area of 256 in², but wants the ratio of the height to the width to remain 1:4. What should the width of the enlarged poster be?

    A.  8

    B.  16

    C.  32

    D.  Not enough information given to solve the problem

**Answer:** C

**Explanation:** To solve this problem, two equations need to be set up.

The first equation relates the area of a rectangular shape to the desired area of the poster.

$$256 = h \times w$$

The second equation relates the desired ratio between the height and the width of the poster.

$$\frac{h}{w} = \frac{1}{4}$$

The second equation can be solved for height in terms of width.

$$h = \frac{1}{4} \times w$$

Substituting the value of h into the first equation and solving for w yields 32 inches.

$$256 = \left(\frac{1}{4} \times w\right) \times w$$

$$256 = \left(\frac{w^2}{4}\right)$$

$$256(4) = w^2$$

$$1024 = w^2$$

$$w = \sqrt{1024} = 32 \text{ inches}$$

## QUESTION 8

After a test, an instructor asked 5 students in the class how many hours they studied for the test. The students' responses are listed in the table below along with their test scores. What function, if any, describes the relationship between the hours studied and the score obtained by the students?

| Student | Hours Studied | Exam Score |
|---------|---------------|------------|
| 1 | 15 | 70 |
| 2 | 20 | 80 |
| 3 | 3 | 46 |
| 4 | 1 | 42 |
| 5 | 30 | 100 |

A. $e(h) = h^2 - 120$

B. $e(h) = 3h + 20$

C. $e(h) = 2h + 40$

D. None of the above

**Answer:** C

**Explanation:** The best approach to this problem is to use the answer choices given to determine if any could model the data supplied.

If 15 hours is substituted for h in answer choice A, a score of 105 results, which is not correct.

If 15 hours is substituted for h in answer choice B, a score of 65 results, which is not correct.

If 15 hours is substituted for h in answer choice C, a score of 70 results, which is correct. If the other 4 data points are tested with this equation, the correct answers result.

## QUESTION 9

If Y is the dependent variable in the tables below, which of the following tables contains values that does not defines a function?

A

| X | Y |
|---|---|
| 5 | 123 |
| 8 | 510 |
| 12 | 1726 |
| 18 | 5830 |
| 23 | 12165 |

B

| X | Y |
|---|---|
| -10 | 15 |
| -5 | 10 |
| 0 | 5 |
| 5 | 10 |
| 10 | 15 |

C

| X | Y |
|---|---|
| -10 | 913 |
| -8 | 457 |
| 0 | -7 |
| 16 | -4391 |
| 24 | -14455 |

D

| X | Y |
|---|---|
| 12 | 114 |
| 20 | 210 |
| 30 | 330 |
| 37 | 414 |
| 37 | 444 |

**Answer:** D

**Explanation:** For a function to be defined, there must be only one unique value of the dependent variable for any value in the domain of the function. In the tables shown above, only answer choice D fails to satisfy this requirement.

## QUESTION 10

What value(s) of x are NOT included in the domain of this function?

$$f(x) = \frac{x^2 + 5x - 14}{x^2 - 7x + 10}$$

A.  $x = -2, x = -5$

B.  $x = 7$

C.  $x = -5$

D.  $x = 2, x = 5,$ and $x = -7$

**Answer:** A

**Explanation:** The domain of a function includes all values of the independent variable which will not result in an undefined value for the dependent variable. Undefined values occur if the denominator of a function is equal to 0. Thus, values of x which are not defined in the domain will include those values of x which result in the denominator equaling to 0. To solve this problem, the denominator is set equal to 0, and the values of x are solved for. $x^2 + 7x + 10 = 0$ results in $x = -2$ and $x = -5$. These two values of x will not be included in the domain of the function.

## QUESTION 11

A cable connects the top of a post with the ground as shown in the figure below. The distance between the base of the tower and the base of the cable is 36 feet, and the cable has an angle of elevation of 35° with respect to the ground.

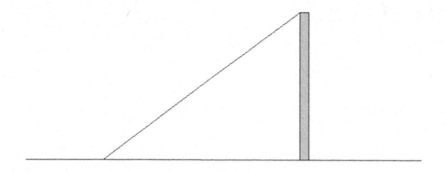

Note: Figure not drawn to scale.

What is the approximate height in feet of the post?

    A.  17

    B.  20

    C.  22

    D.  25

**Answer:** D

**Explanation:** The post is opposite to the angle of 35°. Therefore, one can use the sine function.

$$\sin(35°) = \frac{h}{36}$$

h is the height, and dimensions are in feet.

$$h = 36\sin(35°) = 25.2$$

## QUESTION 12

Which of the following functions cannot be classified as an even function?

    A.  $|x| + 3 = f(x)$

    B.  $x^2 + 3 = f(x)$

    C.  $x^4 + 3 = f(x)$

    D.  $x + 3 = f(x)$

**Answer:** D

**Explanation:** An even function is defined as one in which the substitution of –x for x will result in the same value of the dependent variable as substitution of x would result in. In equation form, this is expressed as $(f(-x) = f(x))$. In the equations shown, substitution of –x into $|x|$, $x^2$, and $x^4$ would result in the same value as substitution of x would result in because the absolute value of a negative number is the positive number and raising a negative number to an even integer results in a positive output. Thus, the only equation which cannot be defined as an even function is in answer choice D.

## QUESTION 13

Given that points I, J, and K represent the midpoints for their respective sides on △ABC, what is the perimeter of triangle ABC?

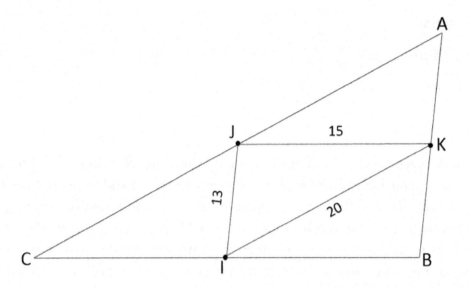

A. 48

B. 72

C. 96

D. 108

**Answer:** C

**Explanation:** The problem states the points I, J, and K were midpoints for their respective sides on △ABC. The line segment formed by points I and K represent a mid-segment, so it will be half of the length of the line segment parallel to it, which is line segment AC. Line segment AC is 2 times the length of line segment IK (20). The same relationships can be used to derive the lengths of line segments BC and AB. The length of AC is 20 × 2=40, length of CB is 15 × 2=30, and length of AB is 13 × 2=26. These three lengths result in a perimeter of 96.

## QUESTION 14

In parallelogram ABCD (not shown), ∡B = x + 15 and ∡C = 3x + 5. Which of the following statements regarding the diagonals of the parallelogram is true?

A. $\overline{BD} = \overline{CA}$

B. $\overline{BD} < \overline{CA}$

C. $\overline{BD} > \overline{CA}$

D. Not enough information given

**Answer:** C

**Explanation:** To understand the relative size of the two diagonals, it is necessary to know the size of the angles of the parallelogram.

The angle measures can be solved for with the given expressions for angles B and C. Angles B and C are consecutive angles in the parallelogram, so they are supplementary with each other. This allows for the two expressions given to be added and set equal to 180°. When this is done, the value of x derived is 40

$$x + 15 + 3x + 5 = 180$$

$$4x + 20 = 180$$

$$4x = 160$$

$$x = 40$$

Substituting 40 into the expressions for angles B and C results in values of 55 and 125, respectively. Thus, in the parallelogram ABCD, Angles C and A are the obtuse angles and Angles B and D are the acute angles. (Angle A is equal to Angle C because they are opposite to one another; this reasoning also explains the equivalence between Angles B and D).

One of the properties of a parallelogram is that the longer diagonal lies opposite the obtuse angle. If the obtuse angle is known to be Angle C, then the diagonal across will be the longer diagonal. This diagonal is line segment DB. Thus, $\overline{BD} > \overline{CA}$.

# QUESTION 15

Which of the following statements accurately describes a rhombus?

    A. The diagonals of the quadrilateral are perpendicular

    B. The diagonals of the quadrilateral are congruent

    C. The diagonals of the quadrilateral bisect one another

    D. A and C

**Answer:** D

**Explanation:** To answer this question, it is necessary to know the properties of a rhombus. The important properties are listed below:

- Consecutive angles are supplementary
- Opposite angles are congruent
- Opposite sides are parallel to one another
- All sides are congruent
- Diagonals bisect the interior angles
- Diagonals are perpendicular bisectors

The last property implies that answer to the problem is D.

# QUESTION 16

Which of the following line segment(s) represents a chord on the circle shown below?

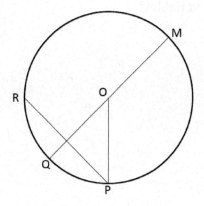

A. $\overline{RP}$

B. $\overline{PO}$

C. $\overline{MQ}$

D. A and C

**Answer:** D

**Explanation:** A chord is defined as a line segment that connects two points on the circumference of a circle. In the circle shown above, Points R and P are on the circumference, and a line segment connects the two points. Points M and Q are also on the circumference, and there is also a line segment that connects those two points. There are two chords shown in the circle, so the correct answer is D.

**QUESTION 17**

Which of the following scatter plots shows that there may be some degree of correlation between the dependent and independent variables?

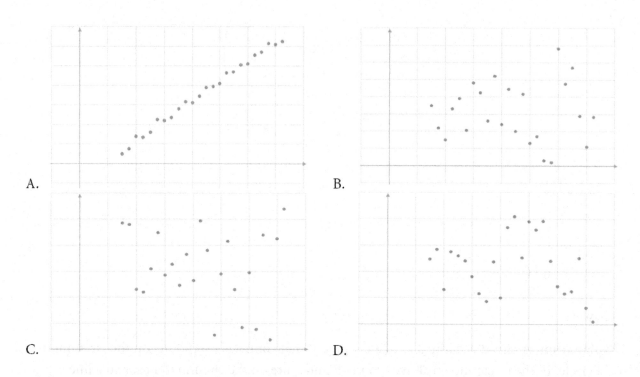

A.

B.

C.

D.

**Answer:** A

**Explanation:** A scatter plot can indicate a relationship among the two variables plotted if the points on the scatter plot line up to show a pattern. This is seen in option A. Option A indicates that as the value of the independent variable increases so will the value of the dependent variable.

**QUESTION 18**

When a six sided standard die is tossed once, what is the probability of getting 1, 3, and a 9?

    A. $\frac{1}{6}$

    B. $\frac{3}{6}$

    C. 0

    D. Undefined

**Answer:** C

**Explanation:** The first step is to list all the possible outcomes of rolling a six sided die. These outcomes are:

$$1 \quad 2 \quad 3 \quad 4 \quad 5 \quad 6$$

Of these outcomes, none of the outcomes have an option of 1, 3, and 9. Each outcome consists of only one single number, so the probability of getting a 1, 3, and a 9 is 0.

NOTE: This question for the probability of getting a 1, 3, and a 9 NOT the probability of getting a 1, 3, or 6.

## QUESTION 19

Sets A and B are defined below. Which of the following sets represents A∩ B?

$$A = \{3, 6, 9, 12, 15, 18\}$$

$$B = \{2, 4, 6, 8, 10, 12, 14\}$$

A. {2, 3, 4, 6, 8, 9, 10, 12, 14, 15, 18}

B. 2, 3, 4, 6, 8, 9, 10, 12, 14, 15, 18

C. {6, 12}

D. A and B

**Answer:** C

**Explanation:** The symbol "∩" implies the intersection of the two sets. The intersection of two sets is defined as a set that contains all elements that both in A and B. In these two sets, the intersection would be set that contains the numbers 6 and 12.

**QUESTION 20**

A set has the following 10 numbers: 12, 19, 25, 28, 54, 26, 87, 23, 98, and 25. If an 11th number is to be added to the set, what does the number have to be in order for the set to have a mean of 40?

    A. -43

    B. 3

    C. 40

    D. 43

**Answer:** D

**Explanation:** For 11 numbers to have a mean of 40, the 11 numbers must add up to a value of 11 × 40=440. Currently, the 10 numbers add up to a value of 397. Thus, the 11th number must be 440 – 397=43.

## QUESTION 21

A data set with a mean of 75 and a standard deviation of 3.5 is known to have a normal distribution. What percent of the data does NOT lie between 71.5 and 78.5?

    A. 99.95

    B. 68.2

    C. 31.8

    D. not enough information given

**Answer:** C

**Explanation:** The problem asks for what percent of the data does NOT lie between 71.5 and 78.5. It is important to note that 71.5 is equal to the mean minus the standard deviation and 78.5 is equal to the mean plus the standard deviation. Thus, the question is asking for the percent of the data that does not lie within one standard deviation of the mean.

In a normal distribution, 68.2% of the data lie within one standard deviation of the mean, which is an important fact to remember. Thus, the answer to the question is 31.8.

**QUESTION 22**

Which of the following ratios is not equal to 68%?

    A. 68:100

    B. 34:50

    C. 102:150

    D. 17:50

**Answer:** D

**Explanation:** Convert each ratio to decimal form to compare directly. All ratios, except D are equivalent to 0.68.

$$\frac{17}{50} = 0.34 = 34\%$$

## QUESTION 23

Solve the following problem:

$$\left(5\text{-}1\times0\text{+}3\div3\right)\times\left(5\text{+}3\times2^4\right)\times\left(\frac{21\times3\times\frac{1}{7}}{5\text{-}1\times4\times3\text{+}2}\right)$$

A.  0

B.  -572.4

C.  -230.4

D.  57.24

**Answer:** B

**Explanation:** To solve this problem, the order of operations needs to be considered. In this problem, there are three separate groups of parenthesis. These must be evaluated in the proper order. The result is shown below:

$$\left(6\right)\times\left(53\right)\times\left(-\frac{9}{5}\right)$$

The next step is evaluating the remaining operations. The result is -572.4.

**QUESTION 24**

Chris' family drove a distance of 300 miles in 2 hours. Pat's family drove a distance of 400 miles in 3 hours. What is the ratio of the speed of Chris' family to the speed of Pat's family?

    A.  9/8

    B.  8/9

    C.  3/4

    D.  2/3

**Answer:** A

**Explanation:** To calculate the ratio between the two speeds, it is important to know the speed of Chris' family and the speed of Pat's family. Speed is taken to be the ratio of distance to time. Chris' family drove 300 miles in 2 hours, so their speed was 150 mph. Pat's family drove 400 miles in 3 hours, so their speed was $\frac{400}{3}$ mph. The ratio of the speed of Chris' family to the speed of Pat's family is $\frac{150}{\frac{400}{3}} = \frac{9}{8}$.

**QUESTION 25**

Which of the following represents the Commutative Property of Multiplication?

    A. $a \times b \times c = a \times b^c$

    B. $a \times b \times c = b \times c \times a$

    C. $a \times b \times c = a \times b \times c$

    D. $a \times b \times c = a + b + c$

**Answer:** B

**Explanation:** The Commutative Property of Multiplication states that the multiplication of numbers does not depend on the order in which the numbers are multiplied. In answer choice B, the order of the numbers is changed, but the numbers remain the same, which demonstrates the commutative property.

## QUESTION 26

What are the values for the domain in the graph shown below?

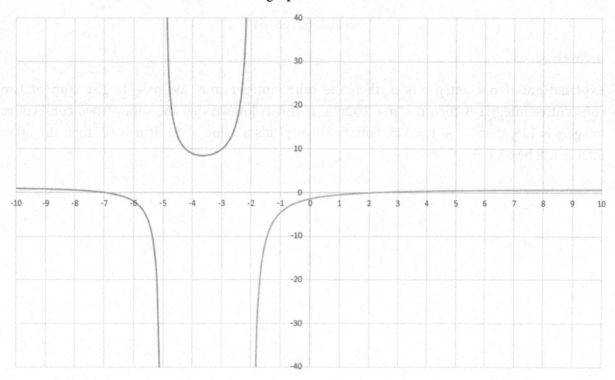

A. [−5, −2]

B. [−∞,−5) U (−5, −2) U (−2, ∞]

C. (−∞,−5) U [−5, −2] U (−2, ∞)

D. None of the above

**Answer:** D

**Explanation:** The graph shows asymptotes at x = −5 and x = −2; these two values cannot be included in the domain for the graph shown above. This eliminates answer choices A and C. Answer choice B is not correct because a parenthesis should be used to for ± ∞ in the interval. Thus, there is no answer given for the domain of this graph. The correct answer would be: (−∞,−5) U (−5, −2) U (−2, ∞)

## QUESTION 27

If the sum of two consecutive integers is 125, then what are the integers?

$$60, 61, 62, 63, 64$$

**Answer:** 62, 63

**Explanation:** If one integer is n, then the other integer must be n + 1. The sum of two consecutive integers is then n + n + 1=2n + 1. If it is known that the sum of two consecutive integers is 125, then 2n + 1 = 125. Solving for n yields a value of 62. If n is 62, then the other integer will be 62 + 1=63.

**QUESTION 28**

Of the following equations, which equation has an x – intercept greater than the y – intercept and a slope equal to the absolute value of the y – intercept.

    A. $y = 2x - 2$

    B. $y = 4x - 16$

    C. $y = 0.5x - 0.5$

    D. A and C

**Answer:** D

**Explanation:** The best approach to this problem is to determine the x – intercept, y – intercept, and slope for each option supplied. In the standard form of a linear equation ($y = mx + b$), b is the y – intercept and m is the slope. The x intercept is calculated by substituting the value of 0 for y and solving for x.

Answer choice A: $m = 2$, $b = -2$, and x – intercept is 1

> This answer is correct because the slope is equal to the absolute value of the y-intercept, and the x-intercept is greater than the y intercept

Answer choice B: $m = 4$, $b = -16$, and x – intercept is 4

> This answer is not correct because slope is not equal to the absolute value of the y intercept.

Answer choice C: $m = 0.5$, $b = -0.5$, and x – intercept is 1

> This answer is correct because the slope is equal to the absolute value of the y-intercept and the x intercept is greater than the y intercept.

Both answer choices A and C satisfy the constraints of the problem statement, so the correct answer is D.

# QUESTION 29

What would be the y-intercept of the graph?

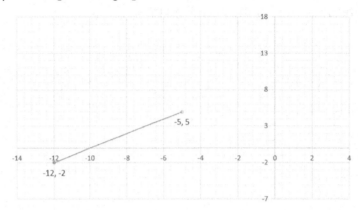

A. 13

B. 10

C. -14

D. -10

**Answer:** B

**Explanation:** The first step is to determine what the equation of the line is.

Since two points are known, the best approach is the point slope formula, which is: $y - y_1 = m \times (x - x_1)$. The variable m is the slope of the line, which can be calculated with the formula shown below.

$$m = \frac{y_2 - y_1}{x_2 - x_1}$$

The slope is calculated to be $\frac{-2 - 5}{-12 - -5} = 1$. Inputting this value for m and the known coordinate values into the point slope formula, the equation of the line is:

$$y-5=1(x-(-5))$$

$$y-5=1(x+5))$$

$$y-5+5=x+5+5$$

$$y=x+10$$

The next step is to determine the y intercept of the line. This is done by inputting a value of 0 for x into the equation of the line. This results in a value of 10. Thus, the y-intercept for a line is 10.

## QUESTION 30

The table below shows the length of time in minutes 25 drivers were stuck in traffic during rush hour. Which of the following values cannot be determined from the data set shown below?

| Time | Number of Drivers |
|---|---|
| 0.0-5.5 | 3 |
| 5.5-15.5 | 10 |
| 15.5-25.5 | 8 |
| 25.5-30.5 | 1 |
| 30.5-45.5 | 3 |

A. range

B. mean

C. median

D. cannot be answered

**Answer:** D

**Explanation:** Without knowing the exact length of time, the range, mean, nor median cannot be calculated. It is necessary to know the exact time each driver was stuck in traffic, to calculate those three values.

## QUESTION 31

A new ice cream store has opened, and the owner of the store has surveyed the first 100 customers. The survey showed that 67 customers have tried their homemade chocolate flavor and 82 customers have tried their homemade vanilla flavor. Of the 100 customers surveyed, 27 customers have tried the homemade vanilla flavor but not the homemade chocolate flavor. How many customers have tried neither the homemade vanilla flavor nor the homemade chocolate flavor?

    A. 6

    B. 12

    C. 40

    D. 55

**Answer:** A

**Explanation:** The best approach to this problem is to construct a Venn diagram. The total entire sample space consists of 100 customers. Of the 100 customers, 27 have tried only the homemade vanilla. It is known that a total of 82 have tried the homemade vanilla, so 55 of the 82 must have tried both homemade vanilla and homemade chocolate. If 55 have tried both homemade chocolate and homemade vanilla, then of the 67 customers who have tried homemade chocolate, 12 of them have tried only homemade chocolate. It is now known that 12 have tried only homemade chocolate, 27 have tried only homemade vanilla, and 55 have tried both homemade vanilla and homemade chocolate. This represents a total of 94 customers who have tried some type of ice cream at the store. Thus, only 6 customers have tried neither the homemade vanilla flavor nor the homemade chocolate flavor.

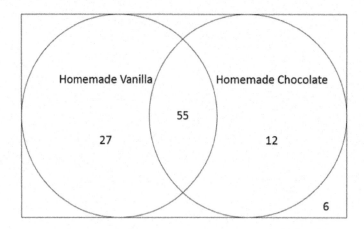

**QUESTION 32**

Mark and his wife are at the grand opening of a car dealership because they each want to win the two prizes that are being raffled away. Every attendee at the grand opening is allowed to write one name on a slip of paper and place that paper into a jar. Each attendee can get one prize. The manager will then select one name from the jar, and this person will have the option of choosing his or her prize. The manger will then select another name from the jar, and this person will take the remaining prize. If Mark and his wife have counted a total of 320 slips in the jar, what is the probability that they will each go home with a prize.

    A. $9.80 \times 10^{-6}$

    B. $6.25 \times 10^{-3}$

    C. $9.77 \times 10^{-6}$

    D. $1.96 \times 10^{-5}$

**Answer:** D

**Explanation:** The problem statement gives enough information to conclude the events of Mark and his wife receiving a prize are dependent because once the first slip is drawn, the number of remaining slips in the jar will decrease.

The first probability necessary to calculate is the probability that either Mark or his wife is called first. The probability the Mark's name will be called in the first raffle is $\frac{1}{320}$. The probability that his wife's name will be called in the first raffle is $\frac{1}{320}$. The probability that Mark or his wife receive the first gift is $\frac{1}{320} + \frac{1}{320} = \frac{2}{320}$. If Mark or his wife are the recipients of the first raffle, then the probability that the other receives the second raffle is $\frac{1}{319}$. The denominator is reduced by 1 because the slip of the first recipient is not replaced back in the jar. The probability that Mark and his wife each go home with a prize is $\frac{2}{320} \times \frac{1}{319} = 1.96 \times 10^{-5}$.

## QUESTION 33

Which of the following events are mutually exclusive?

A. The event of a getting an odd number and an even number when a single card is drawn from a deck.

B. The event of getting a 3 and an odd number when a die is tossed.

C. The event of getting 7 and a number less than 9 when a single card is drawn from a deck.

D. The event of getting a 5 and a number less than 6 when a die is tossed.

**Answer:** A

**Explanation:** To answer this question, it is important to know the definition of mutually exclusive events. Mutually exclusive events are those events which cannot happen simultaneously. To answer this question, it is necessary to determine whether each even in the four options can happen at the same time.

In option A, it is impossible to draw a card that has a number that is both even and odd. Thus, these two events are mutually exclusive, and this is the correct answer.

In option B, it is possible to get a 3 and an odd number when a die is tossed because 3 is an odd number.

In option C, it is possible to get a 7 and a number less than 9 when a single card is drawn because 7 is less than 9.

In option D, it is possible to get 5 and a number less than 6 when a die is tossed because 5 is less than 6.

# QUESTION 34

On a school field trip, Timothy has to choose a walking buddy to accompany him to the vending machine. Of the thirty students he can choose from, 20 are older than him and 10 are younger than him. Of the 20 students older than Timothy, 12 are boys, and of the 10 students younger than him, 6 are girls. What is the probability that Timothy chooses a walking buddy that is older than him or a boy?

A. $\frac{6}{5}$

B. $\frac{2}{3}$

C. $\frac{4}{5}$

D. $\frac{11}{15}$

**Answer:** C

**Explanation:** The first step is to determine whether the events of choosing student older than him and a boy are mutually exclusive. Since there are 12 boys older than Timothy, the two events are not mutually exclusive.

Since the events are not mutually exclusive, the probably that either one may occur is the sum of the probabilities of each occurring separately minus the probably of both happening simultaneously. This can be expressed as:

P (older or boy) = P (older) + P (boy) – P (older and boy)

The probability of selecting a student older than Timothy is $\frac{20}{30} = \frac{2}{3}$

The probability of selecting a student that is a boy is $\frac{16}{30} = \frac{8}{15}$. The 16 resulted from the 12 boys older than him and the 4 boys younger than him.

The probability of selecting an older boy is $\frac{12}{30} = \frac{2}{5}$

Inputting these probabilities into the equation above results in a probability of $\frac{24}{30} = \frac{4}{5}$

## QUESTION 35

Which of the following situations describes dependent events?

    A. The probability of selecting a quarter from a piggy bank and then selecting a penny.

    B. The probability of getting 3 from a single toss of a die and then another 3 from another toss of the die.

    C. The probability of selecting a quarter from a piggy bank and then selecting a penny after the quarter has been put back.

    D. A and C

**Answer:** A

**Explanation:** To solve this problem, the definition of dependent events needs to be known. Dependent events are those events where the outcome of one the events affects the probability of the other event(s).

In option A, the first quarter is not replaced, so when the penny is selected, its sample space is reduced. The sample space for the penny after the selection of the quarter is not the same as the sample space for the selection of the penny without the selection of the quarter before it. Thus, these are dependent events.

In option B, the sample space for tossing a die stays constant and is independent of how many times the die has already been tossed. Thus, these events are not dependent on one another.

In option C, the quarter has been put back into the piggy bank after it has been chosen. The sample space for the penny after the selection of the quarter is the same as the sample space for the selection of the penny before the selection of the quarter. Thus, these events are not dependent on one another.

# QUESTION 36

A shoe store receives a weekly shipment of 100 shoes on Sunday night, so that it can have full inventory to sell from on Monday morning. In a certain week, the store manager was notified that the shipment for that week contained 5 shoes that were damaged due to mishandling. If this notification came Tuesday, and 5 of the 100 delivered shoes were sold the previous day (Monday), what is the probability that at least 1 of the 5 shoes sold was damaged?

A.  0.05

B.  0.230

C.  0.770

D.  0.95

**Answer:** B

**Explanation:** The first step is to determine the number of different ways in which 5 of the 100 shoes can be sold. The counting principle can be used to find this number, but it would be too tedious. The best approach is to use the combinations rule. The combinations rule is used because the order in which the 5 shoes were sold does not matter. The combination rule states that number of possibilities of arranging r objects selected from n objects is calculated by:

$$_nC_r = \frac{n!}{(n\text{-}r)! \times r!}$$

Using the above formula, with $_{100}C_5$, the total number of ways of selling 5 shoes from a total number of 100 shoes is 75,287,520.

To find the probability that at least 1 of the 5 shoes is damaged, it is best to first calculate the probability of zero damaged shoes being sold. If it is known that 5 shoes are damaged, then it is also known that 95 shoes are not damaged. The total number of ways of selling 5 of these 95 shoes is calculated to be 57,940,519 ($_{95}C_5$). The probability of selling 0 damaged shoes is $\frac{57,940,519}{75,287,520}$ =0.770. The probability that at least 1 of the 5 shoes that are sold is damaged is 1 – 0.770=0.230.

Of all the outcomes in the sample space for selling the 5 shoes, there is only one outcome in which at least 1 damaged shoe is not sold, and this outcome is where zero damaged shoes are sold. Thus, subtracting the probability of zero damaged shoes being sold from the probability of the entire sample space (1), the probability of at least one damaged shoe being sold is derived.

## QUESTION 37

Coach Johnson tells his quarterback to stand 50 yards away from the poster shown below, and throw the football at the shaded circle. The intention of this drill is to improve the accuracy of the quarterback's throws. If the quarterback's throw hits the poster, what is the probability that it will hit the shaded circle?

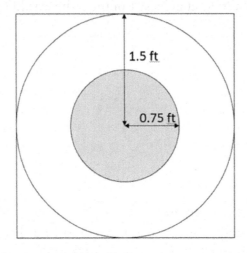

A. 0.196

B. 0.250

C. 0.520

D. 0.785

**Answer:** A

**Explanation:** To answer this question, the area of the poster and the shaded circle need to be known. The area of the poster is the area of a square of length 3 ft; the area is calculated to be 9ft$^2$. The area of the shaded circle is $0.75^2 \times \pi = 1.76715$ ft$^2$. The probability that the football hits the shaded circle is $1.76715/9 = 0.196$.

## QUESTION 38

Of the equations below, which equation does NOT have an x–intercept of 5 and a y–intercept of 15?

    A.  $y = -3x + 15$

    B.  $y + 15 = -2 \times (x - 15)$

    C.  $2y = -6x + 30$

    D.  $y - 9 = -3 \times (x - 2)$

**Answer:** B

**Explanation:** The best approach is to determine the x intercept and y-intercept of each option. The x-intercept is the value of x that will result in a value of 0 for y. The y-intercept is the value of y when x is equal to 0.

The linear equation in option A is written in standard form: $y = mx + b$, were b is the y-intercept. Thus, the y-intercept for option A is 15. The x-intercept is calculated to be 5.

The linear equation in option B is written in point slope form: $y - y_1 = m (x - x_1)$. To determine the y intercept, a value of 0 is substituted for x, and the equation is solved for y. The result is a y intercept of 15. The x-intercept is calculated by substituting 0 for y and solving for x. The result is 7.5. Since the x-intercept is not equal to 5, this is the answer.

**QUESTION 39**

Which of the following line(s) represents an axis of symmetry for $y = 6x^2 + 24x - 24$?

    A.  $x = -2$

    B.  $x = -2$ and $y = -24$

    C.  $x = 2$

    D.  $x = 0$

**Answer:** A

**Explanation:** The axis of symmetry is a line that passes through the vertex of a parabola, and cuts the parabola into two mirror halves. To determine the line of symmetry, it is important to first calculate the vertex of the parabola.

The quadratic equation given is the standard form ($y = ax^2 + bx + c$). The vertex of a parabola given in this form is $-\frac{b}{2a}$. The axis of symmetry will be a vertical line because only a vertical line can equally divide the parabola into two mirror halve. This line of symmetry will be a vertical line passing through the vertex of the parabola, so its equation will be $x = -\frac{b}{2a}$; this is calculated to be $x = -2$.

**QUESTION 40**

Which of the following expressions is equivalent to the expression below?

$$\left(\frac{6\text{-}x}{5x\text{-}30}\right)^{-1} \times \left(\frac{5yx+5y}{10yx+5yx}\right)$$

A. $\frac{(x+1)}{15x}$

B. $\frac{-5y(x+6)}{3x}$

C. $\frac{-5(x+1)}{3x}$

D. $\frac{3(x+1)}{5}$

**Answer:** C

**Explanation:** The first approach is to determine the factors of each expression in the numerators and denominators. This is shown below:

$$\left(\frac{6\text{-}x}{5(x\text{-}6)}\right)^{-1} \times \left(\frac{5y(x+1)}{5yx(2+1)}\right)$$

The next step is to take into account the negative exponent. The best way to handle a negative exponent is to flip entire expression. This is shown below:

$$\left(\frac{5(x\text{-}6)}{6\text{-}x}\right) \times \left(\frac{5y(x+1)}{5yx(2+1)}\right)$$

The next step is to cancel any common factors that are in the numerator and denominator. This is shown below:

$$\left(\frac{5(x\text{-}6)}{6\text{-}x}\right) \times \left(\frac{5\cancel{y}(x+1)}{\cancel{5y}x(2+1)}\right)$$

The expression remaining can be simplified. The simplified result is shown below.

$$\left(\frac{(x\text{-}6)}{6\text{-}x}\right) \times \left(\frac{5(x+1)}{x(2+1)}\right) = \left(\frac{-(6\text{-}x)}{6\text{-}x}\right) \times \left(\frac{5(x+1)}{x(3)}\right) = \left(\frac{-\cancel{(6\text{-}x)}}{\cancel{6\text{-}x}}\right) \times \left(\frac{5(x+1)}{x(3)}\right) = \frac{-5(x+1)}{3x}$$

## QUESTION 41

If the following equation was altered such that b was preceded by a negative sign, h was reduced by –3, and k was increased by 4, then how would the graph of the equation be altered?

$$y = b (x - h)^2 + k$$

A. The graph will shift three units to the left, shift upwards 4 units, and invert.

B. The graph will shift three units to the right and shift upwards 4 units.

C. The graph will shift three units to the right, shift upwards 4 units, and invert.

D. The graph will shift three units to the right, shift downwards 4 units, and invert.

**Answer:** C

**Explanation:** A change in the sign of b will cause the parabola formed by the equation to rotate 180 from its vertex; thus, the graph will invert. A reduction in h by a value of -3 will cause the curve to shift to the right three times (-3 is being subtracted from h, so it leads to an increase in h by 3). An increase in k by a value of 4 will shift the curve upwards 4 units. These transformations are expressed in option C.

## QUESTION 42

Jimmy has obtained a summer job that will last 10 weeks. Jimmy will receive $13 an hour, and will also receive a $200 signing bonus during his first week. If Jimmy plans to work 40 hours each week, which graph shows the cumulative sum of his income throughout the 10 week period?

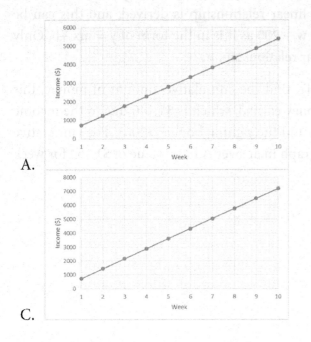

A.

B.

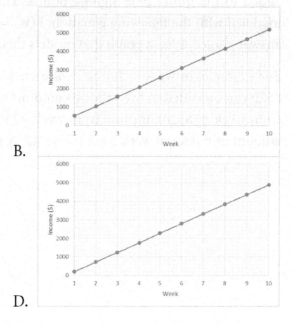

C.

D.

**Answer:** A

**Explanation:** Jimmy will earn a $200 signing bonus in week 1 along with his income for working 40 hours, which will be 40$ × 13=$520. Each following week, Jimmy will work 40 hours, and this amount of work will generate him $520. To obtain the cumulative sum at any week, the amount earned each week should be multiplied by the week under question and this product should be added to the initial 200$ signing bonus. Thus a linear relationship is derived, and this can be modeled with the following equation: i (w) = 520 w + 200 as it is in the form of y = mx +b. Only answer choice A has a graph that models this linear relationship.

For example, in week 3, Jimmy will earn $520. To find the cumulative amount of money, this $520 can be added to the previous amount of money earned, which is $1,240 due to the income from week 1 ($520), income from week 2 ($520), and the signing bonus ($200). The cumulative amount of money at week 3 is $1,760$. Only the graph in answer A has a value of $1,760 for week 3.

## QUESTION 43

If the following curve it shifted three units to the left and two units down, what will be the new equation representing the graph?

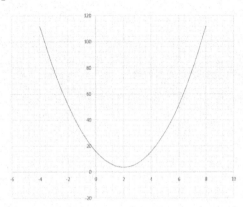

A. $y = 3(x - 2)^2 + 4$

B. $y = 3(x - 5)^2 + 2$

C. $y = 3(x - 3)^2 - 2$

D. $y = 3(x + 1)^2 + 2$

**Answer:** D

**Explanation:** The first step is to determine the equation of the parabola. The form of a quadratic equation is: $y = a(x - h)^2 + k$ or $y = ax^2 + bx + c$. The first form will be used initially because it is easier to represent shifts, which will be explained below. To determine the unique values of a, h, and k, it is best to select three values from the graph and solve a system of three equations. The three points selected are: (0, 16), (2, 4) and (4, 16). Substituting these values for x and y into the equation of a parabola results in:

$$(0, 16): 16 = a \times (0 - h)^2 + k = ah^2 + k = 16$$

$$(2, 4): 4 = a \times (2 - h)^2 + k = ah^2 - 4ah + 4a + k = 4$$

$$(4, 16): 16 = a \times (4 - h)^2 + k = ah^2 - 8ah + 16a + k = 16$$

After solving these equations, the results are a = 3, h = 2, k = 4. Substituting this values in the form of the quadratic equation results in an equation of: $y = 3(x - 2)^2 + 4$.

The questions statement states that the equation will be transformed three units to the left and two units down. When a transformation to the left occurs, the amount of the transformation is subtracted from the value of h. thus a transformation of three units to the left causes the value of h to move to 1. A transformation downward causes the value of k to be reduced by the amount of the transformation. Thus, a transformation of two units downward causes the value of k to reduce to 2. These transformation result in the following equation:  $y = 3 (x + 1)^2 + 2$ .

## QUESTION 44

What function is represented by the graph below?

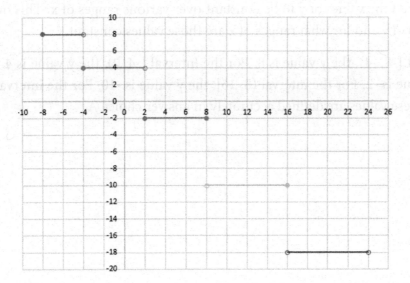

A. $\begin{cases} 8; & -8 \le x < -4 \\ 4; & -4 \le x < 2 \\ -2; & 2 \le x \le 8 \\ -10; & 8 < x \le 16 \\ -18; & 16 < x < 24 \end{cases}$

B. $\begin{cases} 8; & -8 < x < -2 \\ 4; & -4 < x < 2 \\ -2; & 2 < x < 8 \\ -10; & 8 < x < 16 \\ -18; & 16 < x < 24 \end{cases}$

C. $\begin{cases} 8; & -8 \le x \le -2 \\ 4; & -4 \le x \le 2 \\ -2; & 2 \le x \le 8 \\ -10; & 8 \le x \le 16 \\ -18; & 16 \le x \le 24 \end{cases}$

D. $\begin{cases} 8; & -8 < x \le -2 \\ 4; & -4 < x \le 2 \\ -2; & 2 < x < 8 \\ -10; & 8 \le x < 16 \\ -18; & 16 \le x \le 24 \end{cases}$

**Answer:** A

**Explanation:** The graph shown is a representation of a step function. A step function is unique in that it has defined the values of y to be constant over various ranges of x. This question is asking for those values of y and for what ranges of x are those values constant.

For the interval [-8, -4), the y value is 8. For the interval [-4, 2), the y value is 4. For the interval [2, 8], the y value is -2. For the interval (8, 16], the y value is -10. For the interval (-16, 24), the y value is -18. These values are defined accurately in answer choice A.

## QUESTION 45

The following equation can be used to convert between degrees Fahrenheit and degrees Celsius. If it was reported to be 30 degrees Celsius outside, then what is the temperature in degrees Fahrenheit?

$$F^\circ = 32 + \left(^\circ C + \frac{9}{5}\right)$$

    A. 51°

    B. 83°

    C. 86°

    D. 123.8°

**Answer:** C

**Explanation:** Insert 30 into the equation for the temperature in Celsius, and then the equation is evaluated.

$$F^\circ = 32 + \left(30^\circ \times \frac{9}{5}\right)$$

## QUESTION 46

If $a = 2$, $b = 3$, $c = 1$, and $d = 4$, then the expression below is equivalent to what numerical value?

$$a\times(b+c\times a)-b\times c+\frac{d\times d\times a}{c}$$

A. 18

B. 35

C. 39

D. 43

**Answer:** C

**Explanation:** The best approach is to input the values of the variables into the expression and simplify the resulting expression:

$$2\times(3+1\times2)-3\times1+\frac{4\times4\times2}{1}=2\times(3+2)-3\times1+\frac{32}{1}=2\times(5)-3+\frac{32}{1}=10-3+32=39$$

## QUESTION 47

In the figure below, point P bisects line segment $\overline{LN}$. Point O bisects line segment $\overline{LP}$. Point Q bisects line segment $\overline{PN}$. If it is known that line segment $\overline{MP}$ is perpendicular to line segment $\overline{LN}$, then which of the following statements regarding the area of the triangles is true.

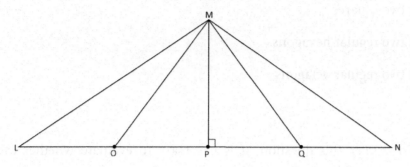

A. △MOP = △MPN

B. △MLO = △MPN

C. △MOP = △MQP = △MLO = △MNQ

D. △MOP > △MLO

**Answer:** C

**Explanation:** The original line segment $\overline{LN}$ has been bisected by point P, so the two resulting line segments will be of equal length: $\overline{LP} = \overline{PN}$. The line segment $\overline{LP}$ has been bisected by Point O, so the two resulting line segments will be of equal length $\overline{LO} = \overline{OP}$. The line segment $\overline{PN}$ has been bisected by Point Q, so the two resulting line segments will be of equal length $\overline{QN} = \overline{PQ}$. Since $\overline{LP} = \overline{PN}$ and both line segments have been bisected, all four resulting line segments will be of equal length: $\overline{LO} = \overline{OP} = \overline{QN} = \overline{PQ}$.

The four triangles that are shown in the picture above have an equal sized base due to the bisecting that was described above. All four triangles also have the same height. The height is the same for all four triangles because the perpendicular distance from the bases to the top of the triangles is the same for all four triangles; this perpendicular distance is $\overline{MP}$. Since the height and the base are the same for all four triangles, the area calculated for all four triangles will be the same. Thus, the correct answer choice is C.

**QUESTION 48**

Which of the following shapes may NOT be similar?

    A. a pair of two isosceles triangles

    B. a pair of two squares

    C. a pair of two regular hexagons

    D. a pair of two regular octagons

**Answer:** A

**Explanation:** To answer this question, it is necessary to evaluate whether each figure in the options given satisfy the following two conditions

- All pairs of corresponding angles are congruent
- All pairs of corresponding sides are proportional

A pair of two isosceles triangles will not always have congruent angles nor will all three corresponding sides have the same ration. A pair of two isosceles triangles may not be similar.

A pair of two squares will have congruent angles (90° each). The corresponding sides will have the same ratio because each square will have the same side lengths.

A pair of two regular hexagons will have congruent angles (120° each). The corresponding sides will have the same ratio because each hexagon will have all the same side lengths.

A pair of two regular octagons will have congruent angles (135° each). The corresponding sides will have the same ratio because each octagon will have all the same side lengths.

## QUESTION 49

A 50ft building casts a shadow that extends a lateral length of 75ft. If a similar building of 150ft tall is in the same area, how far will the shadow extend?

    A.  90.1ft

    B.  150ft

    C.  225ft

    D.  270.5ft

**Answer:** C

**Explanation:** To answer this questions, it is important to know that the triangles that are formed by the shadow and the building are similar. The ratio between the heights of the buildings will be the same as the ratio between the lengths of the shadows. The buildings have a ratio of $\frac{150}{50}$ =3. The lengths of the shadow must be of the same ratio, so the shadow casts by the taller building will be 75ft × 3=225ft.

It can be completed in a simpler way by using proportions:

$$\frac{50}{75} = \frac{150}{x}$$

Solve for x:

$$50(x)=150(75)$$

$$50x=11250$$

$$x=225$$

**QUESTION 50**

Which of the following statements defines the conditions necessary for shapes to be similar?

A. all pairs of corresponding angles are congruent

B. all pairs of corresponding sides are proportional

C. all pairs of corresponding angles and sides are congruent

D. A and B

**Answer:** D

**Explanation:** To answer this question it is necessary to know what properties define similar polygons:

- all pairs of corresponding angles are congruent
- all pairs of corresponding sides are proportional

## QUESTION 51

A soda can has a total surface area of $35\pi$ in². If the height of the right circular cylinder is 2 inches greater than the radius of the circular base, what is the length of the diameter of the circular base?

A. 10.0 inches

B. 8.4 inches

C. 6.6 inches

D. 5.0 inches

**Answer:** D

**Explanation:** The formula for the total surface area of a right circular cylinder, which is taken to be the shape of the soda can, is shown below:

$$\text{Total Surface Area}=2\pi rh+2\pi r^2$$

The problem statement says the height, h, is 2 inches greater than the radius. This can be expressed as:

$$h=r+2$$

Substituting the expression for h into the equation for the total surface area can yield the value of the radius because the total surface area is known. Solving the equation below yields a radius of 2.5 inches, which translates to a diameter of 5 inches.

$$35\pi=2\pi r\times(r+2)+2\pi r^2$$

Remove $\pi$ as each term has $\pi$ on both sides of the equal sign.

$$35=2r\times(r+2)+2r^2$$

$$\frac{35}{2}=r^2+2r+r^2$$

$$2r^2+2r-\frac{35}{2}=0$$

$$r=\frac{5}{2}=2/5$$

$$d=5$$

## QUESTION 52

An ice cream store owner purchases ice cream from a vendor in 5 gallon buckets. He sells this ice cream in cones to his customers. When selling the ice cream, the owner fills the cone with ice cream and adds an extra scoop of the ice cream on the top. Each cone has a height of 7 inches and a circular base of diameter 4 inches. The extra scoop of ice cream is in the shape of a hemisphere with a radius 2 inches. If the owner purchases cones in packages of 10, how many packages are needed for every bucket of ice cream bought? (Assume the cone has the shape of a right circular cone. Also, 7.48 gal = 1 ft³)

A.  1 package

B.  2 packages

C.  3 packages

D.  4 packages

**Answer:** C

**Explanation:** The first step is to calculate the volume of the ice cream that can be sold in one cone.

The formula for a cone is shown below. All of the necessary parameters to calculate the volume are given; the height is 7 inches and the radius is 2 inches. Using these parameters, a volume of 29.32 in³ is calculated.

$$\text{Volume of Cone} = \frac{1}{3} \times \pi \times r^2 \times h$$

The formula for a hemisphere is shown below. All of the necessary parameters to calculate the volume are given; the radius is 2 inches. Using this radius, a volume of 16.76 in³ is calculated.

$$\text{Volume of Hemisphere} = \frac{1}{2}\left(\frac{4}{3} \times \pi \times r^3\right)$$

The total volume of ice cream that can be sold in one cone is 46.08 in³.

It is necessary to convert this volume from inches³ to gallons. This will be done with the given unit conversion and also the known fact that 12 inches = 1 ft. The unit conversion is shown below.

$$\frac{7.48 \text{ gal}}{1 \text{ ft}^3} \times \left(\frac{1 \text{ ft}}{12 \text{ in}}\right)^3 = \frac{7.48 \text{ gal}}{1728 \text{ in}^3}$$

Multiplying the known volume (46.08 in³) in in³ by $\frac{7.48 \text{ gal}}{1728 \text{ in}^3}$ yields the volume of the cone to be approximately 0.200 gal.

Now that the volume of ice cream in a cone is known, the next step is to calculate how many cones can be sold from a 5 gallon bucket. This is calculated by dividing 5 gallons by the volume of the cone (0.200 gal). The result is 25.07 cones, which rounds down to 25 cones. The question asks for how many packages of cones are need to be bought per bucket of ice cream. This can be calculated by dividing 25 cones by 10 cones (the number of cones per package). The result is rounded up to 3 packages.

**QUESTION 53**

Which of the following properties regarding circles is not true?

    A. A line tangent to the circle only touches the circle at one point.

    B. A line secant to the circle joints two points on the circumference.

    C. A central angle of a circle is an angle in which the vertex lies at the center of the circle and its sides are radii of the circle.

    D. Concentric circles must be congruent to one another.

**Answer:** D

**Explanation:** To solve this problem correctly, the following definitions needs to be known. These definitions will show that D is the correct answer to the problem.

- Concentric circles: circles that lie on the same plane and have a common center, but have difference size.
- Central angle: an angle who vertex lies at the center of the circle and whose sides are radii of the circle
- Tangent: a line that intersects a circle at only one point
- Secant: a line that intersects a circle at two points

## QUESTION 54

What is the distance between points (3, -9) and (4, 8)?

**Answer:** 17.03

**Explanation:** This is a simple application of the distance formula, which is shown below:

$$d=\sqrt{(x_2-x_1)^2+(y_2-y_1)^2}$$

Using the two knowing data points, the distance is calculated to be:

$$d=\sqrt{(3-4)^2+(-9-8)^2} = \sqrt{290}$$

A calculator can be used to determine the value of $\sqrt{290}$; the answer is approximately 17.03.

The median of the data set is also known as the second quartile of the data set. The median is calculated to be 8.5 minutes.

The value of the first quartile can be calculated by taking the median of the values in the data set smaller than the value of the second quartile. This results in value of 3.5 minutes for the first quartile.

The value of the third quartile can be calculated by taking the median of the values in the data set larger than the value of the second quartile. This results in value of 14.5 minutes for the first quartile.

With these known values, it becomes obvious that the correct box plot is shown in option B.

## QUESTION 55

The governor of a Ohio was given a report of the number of parks in each county within the state. After looking at the report, the governor became curious about certain data points. If the following numbers were in the report, which numbers most likely caught the governor's attention?

| County | 1 | 2 | 3 | 4 | 5 | 6 | 7 | 8 | 9 | 10 | 11 | 12 | 13 | 14 | 15 | 16 | 17 | 18 | 19 | 20 |
|---|---|---|---|---|---|---|---|---|---|---|---|---|---|---|---|---|---|---|---|---|
| Number of Parks | 7 | 8 | 6 | 5 | 9 | 5 | 5 | 5 | 6 | 6 | 7 | 1 | 0 | 15 | 8 | 8 | 6 | 5 | 6 | 7 |

    A. County 12, 13, 14

    B. County 13

    C. County 14

    D. County 4, 6, 7, 8, and 18

**Answer:** A

**Explanation:** This questions is asking to identify the outliers in a given data set. Outliers are those values that have a value that is very different from the common values of the data set. In this data set, the common values are within the range of 5 to 9 parks. Thus, the 1 park in County 12, the absence of parks in County 13, and the 15 parks in County are the outliers of the data set.

# Practice Test 3

This page is intentionally left blank.

## Exam Answer Sheet – Test 3

Below is an optional answer sheet to use to document answers.

| Question Number | Selected Answer | Question Number | Selected Answer |
|---|---|---|---|
| 1 | | 31 | |
| 2 | | 32 | |
| 3 | | 33 | |
| 4 | | 34 | |
| 5 | | 35 | |
| 6 | | 36 | |
| 7 | | 37 | |
| 8 | | 38 | |
| 9 | | 39 | |
| 10 | | 40 | |
| 11 | | 41 | |
| 12 | | 42 | |
| 13 | | 43 | |
| 14 | | 44 | |
| 15 | | 45 | |
| 16 | | 46 | |
| 17 | | 47 | |
| 18 | | 48 | |
| 19 | | 49 | |
| 20 | | 50 | |
| 21 | | 51 | |
| 22 | | 52 | |
| 23 | | 53 | |
| 24 | | 54 | |
| 25 | | 55 | |
| 26 | | | |
| 27 | | | |
| 28 | | | |
| 29 | | | |
| 30 | | | |

This page is intentionally left blank.

## QUESTION 1

The division of $2x^2+14x+24$ by the sum of $2x$ and $2x^2+6x$ results in which of the following expressions?

    A. $\dfrac{(x+3)}{x}$

    B. $\dfrac{(x+3)}{2x}$

    C. $\dfrac{(x+4)}{2}$

    D. $\dfrac{(x+4)}{x}$

**Answer:**

**QUESTION 2**

If $(x \odot y) = (4x^3 + 12 + 12y + 6y^2)$, then what expression is equivalent to $(4x) \odot 12$?

    A.  $256x^3 + 1020$

    B.  1276

    C.  $64x^3 + 1020$

    D.  $16x + 1020$

**Answer:**

**QUESTION 3**

The point A for the following graph represents what point?

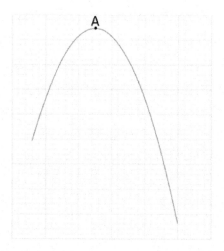

    A.  minimum

    B.  maximum

    C.  vertex

    D.  B and C

**Answer:**

198

## QUESTION 4

What is the range and domain of the function shown below?

$$y = |x+3| - 5$$

A. Domain: all real numbers; Range: all real numbers

B. Domain: all real numbers; Range: all real numbers greater than -5

C. Domain: all real numbers except -3; Range: all real numbers greater than -5

D. Domain: all positive real numbers; Range: all positive real numbers

**Answer:**

## QUESTION 5

In what intervals of the domain shown below does the graph increase?

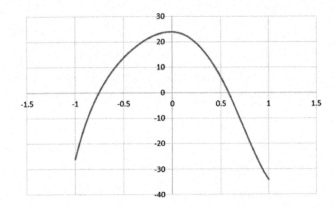

A. [0,1]

B. [-1,1]

C. [-0.75, 0.55]

D. [-1, 0]

**Answer:**

## QUESTION 6

When the grocery store opens, a store manager tells an employee to take half of the cans off of a shelf. In the first four hours of the store opening, 12 customers each bought 3 cans from the shelf. The manager then told the employee to return the cans he removed earlier back to the shelf. Before the store closed, 10 new customers each bought 5 cans from the shelf. When the store was closing, the manager saw that only two cans remained on the shelf. How many cans did the employee originally remove from the shelf?

    A.  88

    B.  44

    C.  25

    D.  18

**Answer:**

## QUESTION 7

What is the value of p in the figure below?

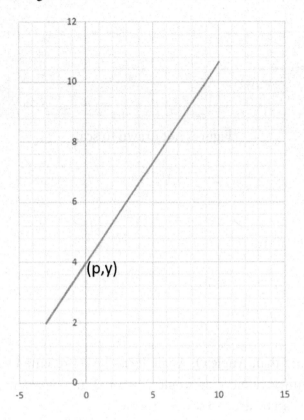

(p,y)

A. -4

B. 2/3

C. 0

D. 4

**Answer:**

## QUESTION 8

Which of the following shapes has the largest area?

  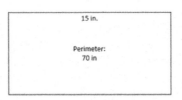 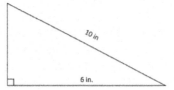

Figures not drawn to scale

A. Circle

B. Square

C. Rectangle

D. Triangle

**Answer:**

## QUESTION 9

Angle P is 24 degrees more than Angle Q. Angle P can be represented with variable x, and Angle Q can be represented with variable y. If Angles P and Q are supplementary, then which of the following set of equation can be used to solve for x and y?

A. $x + y = 90°$

$2y + 24 = 90°$

B. $x + y = 180°$

$2y + 24 = 180°$

C. $x + y = 180°$

$2x + 24 = 180°$

D. $x + y = 90°$

$2x + 24 = 90°$

**Answer:**

**QUESTION 10**

Which of the following equations will be perpendicular to the following graph?

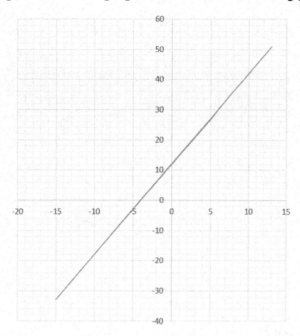

A. $y = 3x + 12$

B. $y = -\frac{1}{3}x + 9$

C. $y = \frac{1}{3}x + 12$

D. $y = \frac{1}{3}x - 12$

**Answer:**

**QUESTION 11**

In the figure below $\overleftrightarrow{AB} \parallel \overrightarrow{CD}$ and ∢EKA > ∢GIA, which of the following statements is NOT true?

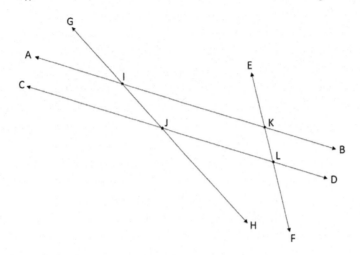

A. ∢GIB > ∢AKF

B. ∢GJD = ∢ CJH

C. ∢EKB + ∢AKF + ∢BKF + ∢EKA = 360°

D. ∢EKB = ∢GJD

**Answer:**

**QUESTION 12**

The radius of a right circular cylinder is increased by 200%. What is the ratio of the volume of the cylinder after the expansion to the volume of the cylinder before the expansion?

A. 0.5

B. 1.33

C. 2

D. 4

**Answer:**

## QUESTION 13

A student draws a perfect regular pentagon on a piece of paper using a ruler and a protractor. After drawing the polygon, the student measures the angle at one corner to be 105°. What is the percent error of this measurement?

A. 2.78%

B. 2.86%

C. 3%

D. 45.8%

**Answer:**

## QUESTION 14

A newly designed battery is shaped as rectangular prism with dimensions of 40.3 mm by 21.2 mm by 8.3 mm. If 10 of these batteries weigh 7.48 x 10³ mg, then what is the density of the newly designed battery in mg/mm³?

A. 0.105

B. 1.05

C. 9.48

D. 10.5

**Answer:**

## QUESTION 15

Which of the following is NOT a continuous variable?

A. number of chairs in a classroom

B. temperature in a classroom

C. weight of the students in a classroom

D. height of the students in a classroom

**Answer:**

## QUESTION16

Which of the following is true if $\overleftrightarrow{AB} \parallel \overleftrightarrow{CD}$, $\overleftrightarrow{EF} \parallel \overleftrightarrow{GH}$, $\overrightarrow{KI}$ bisects ∢AKF, and $\overrightarrow{JL}$ bisects ∢ALH?

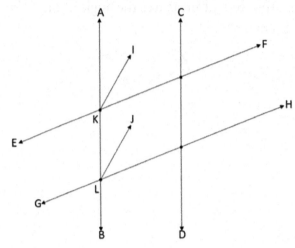

A.  ∢AKI + ∢IKF = ∢GLB

B.  ∢AKI > ∢IKF

C.  ∢AKE = ∢AKF

D.  ∢EKB = ∢AKI

**Answer:**

## QUESTION 17

There are 20 people participated in a clinical research trial for a new pill that claims to help people lose weight. Every week, the lab assistants record the weights of the 20 people. The data below shows the weight loss for the 20 people after 10 weeks of the research trial. What is the mode, mean, median, and range for the data set?

| Stem | Leaf |
|------|------|
| 0 | 6  8  8  9 |
| 1 | 1  2  4  5  5  8  8  8 |
| 2 | 0  1  1  5  6  8  9 |
| 3 | 0 |

A. Mode = 18, Mean = 17.6, Median = 18, Range = 24

B. Mode = 8, Mean = 5.1, Median = 8, Range = 9

C. Mode = 1, Mean = 1.5, Median = 1.5, Range = 3

D. Mode = 10, Mean = 15, Median = 15, Range = 30

**Answer:**

## QUESTION 18

The perimeter of a heptagon is 180 and the lengths of the sides are in the ratio 1:3:5:7:8:9:12. What is the measure of the longest side of the heptagon?

A. 4

B. 25.7

C. 48

D. 45

**Answer:**

207

## QUESTION 19

The following figure shows a hexagonal prism separated into its 8 faces. If the height of the rectangles is 24 cm and the width of the rectangles is 8 cm, then what is the total surface area of the hexagonal prism?

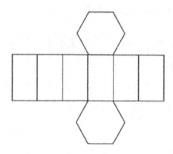

    A.  1484.56 cm$^2$

    B.  1152 cm$^2$

    C.  358.28 cm$^2$

    D.  332.56 cm$^2$

**Answer:**

# QUESTION 20

A mother was looking for a daycare in her city to send her child. She came across 50 different daycares, each with a different hourly cost. The following histogram summarizes the costs of the daycares. Which of the following statements regarding the mean, mode, and median are true?

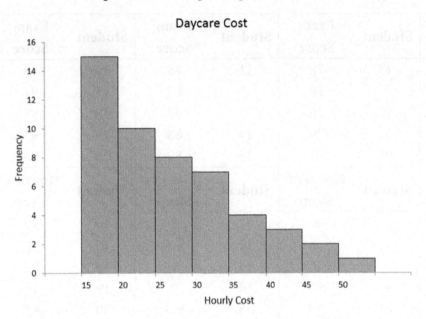

A. Mode < Median < Mean

B. Mean = Mode = Median

C. Mean < Median < Mode

D. Not enough information given

**Answer:**

## QUESTION 21

Mrs. Garcia asked her students how many hours they slept every school night. She then took this data and compared it with the grades those students earned on their first exam. The two separate sets of data are shown below. Which of the following scatter plots best models the data sets?

| Student | Exam Score | Student | Exam Score | Student | Exam Score | Student | Exam Score | Student | Exam Score |
|---------|-----------|---------|-----------|---------|-----------|---------|-----------|---------|-----------|
| 1 | 55 | 6 | 78 | 11 | 85 | 16 | 89 | 21 | 97 |
| 2 | 58 | 7 | 78 | 12 | 85 | 17 | 91 | 22 | 98 |
| 3 | 62 | 8 | 79 | 13 | 87 | 18 | 95 | 23 | 99 |
| 4 | 74 | 9 | 79 | 14 | 88 | 19 | 95 | 24 | 100 |
| 5 | 75 | 10 | 84 | 15 | 89 | 20 | 96 | 25 | 100 |

| Student | Hours of Sleep | Student | Hours of Sleep | Student | Hours of Sleep | Student | Hours of Sleep | Student | Hours of Sleep |
|---------|---------------|---------|---------------|---------|---------------|---------|---------------|---------|---------------|
| 1 | 12 | 6 | 8 | 11 | 8 | 16 | 8.5 | 21 | 8 |
| 2 | 2 | 7 | 8 | 12 | 8.5 | 17 | 8 | 22 | 7.5 |
| 3 | 10 | 8 | 9 | 13 | 9 | 18 | 7.5 | 23 | 8 |
| 4 | 5 | 9 | 8.5 | 14 | 9 | 19 | 10 | 24 | 7.5 |
| 5 | 5 | 10 | 7.5 | 15 | 9.5 | 20 | 8.5 | 25 | 6 |

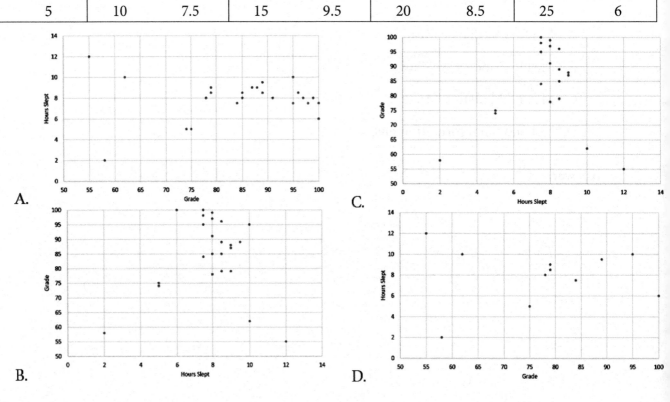

A.

B.

C.

D.

**Answer:**

210

## QUESTION 22

A high school club plans to sell chocolate chip cookies for a fundraising event. The club has $125 to invest in ingredients. One box contains 20 ounces of cookie dough and costs $20, and one package of chocolate chips costs $3. If x ounces of cookie dough and y packages of chocolate chips are needed, which of the following inequalities can be used to model the possible number of ounces of cookie dough and chocolate chips packages that can be bought?

    A. $20x+3y\geq125$

    B. $20x+3y\leq125$

    C. $\frac{20}{x}+\frac{3}{y}>125$

    D. $\frac{20}{x}-\frac{3}{y}>125$

**Answer:**

## QUESTION 23

If $-\frac{4}{5}<2t+5<\frac{5}{2}$, what is one possible value of $6t+15$?

    A. -4

    B. -3

    C. 6

    D. 8

**Answer:**

## QUESTION 24

In a laboratory experiment, the population of mice M doubles every 15 days. It is reported that the experiment starts out with 20 mice. Assuming no mice die during the experiment, which of the following equations represents the number of mice after d days?

    A. $20+2^{\frac{d}{15}}$

    B. $20+2^{d}$

    C. $2(20)^{\frac{d}{15}}$

    D. $20(2)^{\frac{d}{15}}$

**Answer:**

## QUESTION 25

If the $\frac{6x^2}{3x+1}$ is written in form $\frac{1}{3x+1}+A$, what is A in terms of x?

   A. $2x-\frac{2}{3}$

   B. $3x-1$

   C. $2x^2-1$

   D. $6x^2-1$

**Answer:**

## QUESTION 26

A car rental company charges $10.00 per day plus tax for a basic automobile. The tax rate is 8.25%, and the company also charges a one-time untaxed fee of $75.00. If a person rents a basic automobile for x days and spends $120 dollars in gas, which of the following represents the amount of money spent by this person?

   A. $1.0825(10.00x)+195$

   B. $(10.00+8.25x)+195$

   C. $1.0825(10.00x+195)$

   D. $8.25(10.00x)+195$

**Answer:**

## QUESTION 27

$$\frac{1-\dfrac{1}{\sqrt{3}}}{1+\dfrac{1}{\sqrt{3}}}$$

What is the expression above equivalent to?

   A. $1+\sqrt{3}$

   B. $2-\sqrt{3}$

   C. $1+2\sqrt{3}$

   D. $\frac{2}{3}$

**Answer:**

**QUESTION 28**

A marketing company conducted a survey to determine the preference of different chips among five different age groups. The table below displays a summary of the survey results.

| Age Group (years old) | Preference | | |
|---|---|---|---|
| | Potato Chips | Corn Chips | Plantain Chips |
| 10-19 | 32 | 13 | 15 |
| 20-29 | 18 | 16 | 16 |
| 30-39 | 12 | 22 | 16 |
| 40-49 | 10 | 13 | 17 |
| 50-59 | 11 | 15 | 24 |
| Total | 83 | 79 | 88 |

According to the table, for which age group did the greatest percentage of people report they prefer corn chips?

A.  20-29 years old

B.  30-39 years old

C.  40-49 years old

D.  50-59 years old

**Answer:**

## QUESTION 29

A kid plans to sell cups of lemonade in order to raise money for a birthday present. He has determined the cost for n cups of lemonade is modeled by the equation c=0.5n+18. Each cup of lemonade sells for $2, and the kid makes a profit when the money collected from the amount of cups sold exceeds the cost. Which of the following inequalities gives all possible values of n for which the kid will make a profit?

A. n<12

B. n>12

C. n<18

D. n>18

**Answer:**

## QUESTION 30

A fuel tank is one-quarter full when it has 6 gallons. After adding $20 worth of fuel, the tank is two-thirds full. In addition, the fuel price in dollars is $3.20 per gallon. If the car runs at 25 miles per gallon when going at an average speed of 50 miles/hour, which of the following functions, f, models the number of gallons of gas remaining in the tank t hours?

A. $f(t)=16-\dfrac{50}{25}t$

B. $f(t)=24-\dfrac{25}{50}t$

C. $f(t)=\dfrac{16-50t}{25}$

D. $f(t)=\dfrac{24-25t}{50}$

**Answer:**

## QUESTION 31

According to an article in a financial magazine, a company had an income of 3.6 billion dollars during the previous year. Based on this report, Kirk estimates that the company earned an average of 3 million dollars per month. Which of the following statements best describes Kirk's estimate for the company's average monthly income?

    A.  The estimate is low by a factor of 10.

    B.  The estimate is high by a factor of 10.

    C.  The estimate is low by a factor of 100.

    D.  The estimate is high by a factor of 100.

**Answer:**

## QUESTION 32

$$24x = 9y - 15 - 3x$$

What is the x-intercept of the equation above?

    A.  $-\dfrac{5}{9}$

    B.  $-\dfrac{3}{8}$

    C.  $\dfrac{1}{3}$

    D.  $\dfrac{5}{8}$

**Answer:**

**QUESTION 33**

Which of the following describes the graph of $y=\frac{1}{3}f(x)$ in the interval $0 \le x \le \infty$ if $f(x)=x^2$?

    A.  increases more rapidly

    B.  increases more slowly

    C.  decreases more rapidly

    D.  decreases more slowly

**Answer:**

**QUESTION 34**

A store sells toy cars for \$4 and toy trucks for \$6. The day before New Year's Day, the store sold 10 more cars than trucks and earns \$260. Which system of equations could be used to find the number of cars C and trucks T that the store sold that day?

    A.  C+T=10 and 4C+6T=260

    B.  C-T=10 and 4C+6T=260

    C.  C+10T=260 and 4C-6T=0

    D.  10C-T=0 and 4C-6T=100

**Answer:**

**QUESTION 35**

What is the area of the shaded region? (The hexagon shown is a regular hexagon)

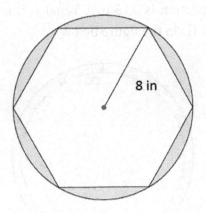

8 in

A. 201.06 inches

B. 166.28 inches

C. 34.79 inches

D. 9.06 inches

**Answer:**

# QUESTION 36

An aerial view of segment of drill pipe is shown below. The outer diameter of the drill pipe is 22.5 inches. The area of the shaded portion is 83.5 in² . What is the inner diameter of the drill pipe? (The inner diameter is labeled as ID in the figure below)

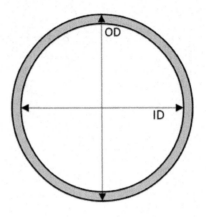

A.  10 in

B.  13.13 in

C.  20 in

D.  21.9 in

**Answer:**

**QUESTION 37**

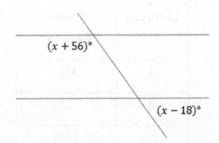

In the figure above, there are two parallel horizontal lines crossed by slanted line. What is the value of x?

A. 67

B. 68

C. 70

D. 71

**Answer:**

**QUESTION 38**

| Element | Mass Percent |
|---------|--------------|
| A | 35% |
| B | 20% |
| C | 45% |

The table above shows the percent composition of mass of the elements in a chemical compound. If element A weighs 14 grams by itself, what is the weight of the element C in grams?

   A. 10

   B. 16

   C. 18

   D. 40

**Answer:**

**QUESTION 39**

The minute hand of a clock makes one quarter of a circumference as 15 minutes pass. What angle, in degrees, does the hour hand move?

   A. 7.5

   B. 15.0

   C. 28.0

   D. 30.0

**Answer:**

**QUESTION 40**

There are four consecutive numbers. The last number is equal to the sum of half of the first number, one-third of the second number, and one-fourth of the third number. What is the first number?

A. 22

B. 23

C. 25

D. 26

**Answer:**

**QUESTION 41**

Select all the appropriate zeros for the function $x^3 - 6x^2 + 11x - 6$.

$$3 \quad 2 \quad 1 \quad -1 \quad 2 \quad 0 \quad 3$$

**Answer:**

**QUESTION 42**

Which of the following options can be solutions to the inequality: $|3x + 9| < 5x + 7$?

$$-3 \quad -5 \quad 1 \quad 3 \quad 5$$

**Answer:**

**QUESTION 43**

Which of the following numbers can be the length of the third side of a triangle, whose other two sides are 10 and 14?

$$3 \quad 5 \quad 12 \quad 18 \quad 25$$

**Answer:**

**QUESTION 44**

If a triangle has a known angle of 32, which of the following pairs of numbers can be the measurements of the two other angles?

52 and 96     90 and 45     79 and 116     45 and 60     116 and 32

**Answer:**

**QUESTION 45**

Which of the following numbers are considered real numbers?

$$0.75 \quad 0 \quad 10 \quad -28 \quad \sqrt{-2}, \quad \sqrt{-25}$$

**Answer:**

**QUESTION 46**

Five friends go to a donut shop. John orders 6 donuts. Mary orders 150% more donuts than John. Carol orders 3 more donuts than Mary. Hector orders 25% of the donuts Carol orders. Eric orders 2 more donuts than Hector. Which of the following people ordered more than 5 donuts?

John   Mary   Carol   Hector Eric

**Answer:**

**QUESTION 47**

Which of the following numbers is greater than 125 but less than 875?

    A. -126

    B. $1.25 \times 10^2$

    C. $\frac{875}{10}$

    D. $125 \times \sqrt{2}$

**Answer:**

**QUESTION 48**

If the multiplicative inverse of 1/5 is divided by the additive inverse of -5, what is the result?

    A. 0

    B. 1

    C. -1

    D. 25

**Answer:**

**QUESTION 49**

What is the greatest common factor of 36 and 54?

    A. 1944

    B. 108

    C. 18

    D. 9

**Answer:**

**QUESTION 50**

$$x^2+y^2+4x-10y=7$$

The equation of a circle in the xy-plane is shown above. What is the diameter of the circle?

**Answer:**

**QUESTION 51**

The function f is defined by $f(x)=x^3-x^2-14x+c$, where c is a constant. In the xy-plane, the graph of f intersects the x-axis at the three points (2,0), (3,0) and (p,0). What is the value of c?

    A. -4

    B. 12

    C. 24

    D. 32

**Answer:**

## QUESTION 52

Which of the following could be the graph of y=2x-3?

A.

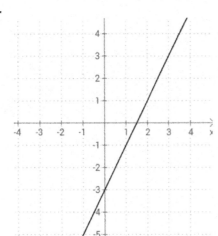

C.

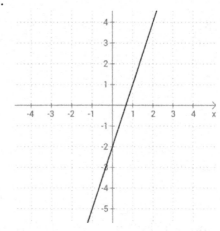

B.

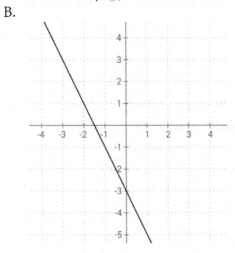

D.

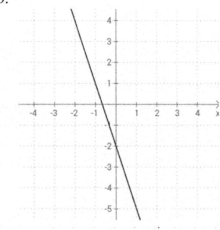

**Answer:**

**QUESTION 53**

A line is graphed in the xy-plane below.

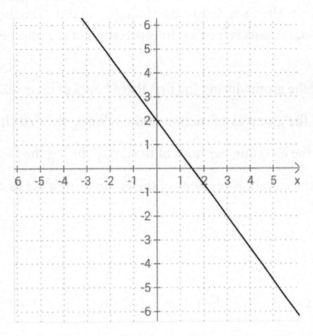

If the line is translated down 2 units and right 8 units, then what is the slope of the new line?

A. -4

B. $-\frac{4}{3}$

C. $-\frac{1}{4}$

D. $\frac{1}{4}$

**Answer:**

**QUESTION 54**

The elevation h in feet as a function of time of a group of hikers as they hike in a mountain is described by h=736t+3210. The variable t is time in hours, and the function is valid when 0<t<3. Which of the following statements is the best interpretation of the number 736 in the context of this problem?

    A. The elevation of the group during the first three hours of their hike.

    B. The elevation of the group as a function of time during the first three hours of their hike.

    C. The decrease in the elevation per hour of the group during the first three hours of hiking.

    D. The increase in the elevation per hour of the group during the first three hours of hiking.

**Answer:**

**QUESTION 55**

If $a^{\frac{1}{3}}=y$, where a>0 and y>0, which of the following equations gives a in terms of y?

    A. $a=-y^3$

    B. $a=\frac{1}{y^3}$

    C. $a=-\frac{1}{y^3}$

    D. $a=y^3$

**Answer:**

# Middle School Practice Exam Answers – Test 3

Below is an optional answer sheet to use to document answers.

| Question Number | Selected Answer | Question Number | Selected Answer |
|---|---|---|---|
| 1 | A | 31 | C |
| 2 | A | 32 | A |
| 3 | D | 33 | B |
| 4 | B | 34 | B |
| 5 | D | 35 | C |
| 6 | B | 36 | C |
| 7 | C | 37 | D |
| 8 | C | 38 | C |
| 9 | B | 39 | A |
| 10 | B | 40 | D |
| 11 | D | 41 | 3,2,1 |
| 12 | D | 42 | 3,5 |
| 13 | A | 43 | 5,12,18 |
| 14 | A | 44 | 52 and 96; 116 and 32 |
| 15 | A | 45 | 0.75,010,-28 |
| 16 | A | 46 | John, Mary, and Carol |
| 17 | A | 47 | D |
| 18 | C | 48 | B |
| 19 | A | 49 | C |
| 20 | A | 50 | $6\sqrt{3}$ |
| 21 | B | 51 | C |
| 22 | B | 52 | A |
| 23 | C | 53 | B |
| 24 | D | 54 | D |
| 25 | B | 55 | B |
| 26 | A | | |
| 27 | B | | |
| 28 | B | | |
| 29 | B | | |
| 30 | A | | |

This page is intentionally left blank.

## QUESTION 1

The division of $2x^2+14x+24$ by the sum of $2x$ and $2x^2+6x$ results in which of the following expressions?

A. $\frac{(x+3)}{x}$

B. $\frac{(x+3)}{2x}$

C. $\frac{(x+4)}{2}$

D. $\frac{(x+4)}{x}$

**Answer:** A

**Explanation:** The first step is to take the sum of $2x$ and $2x^2 + 6x$, which is equal to $2x^2 + 8x$. To proceed with the division, it best to write the division in fractional form, shown below:

$$\frac{2x^2 + 14x +24}{2x^2 + 8x}$$

The second step is to determine the factors of both the numerator and denominator. Once the factors are derived, the next step is to cancel any common factors present in both the numerator and denominator. This is shown below:

$$\frac{2(x^2 + 7x +12)}{2(x^2 + 4x)} = \frac{\cancel{2}(x^2 + 7x +12)}{\cancel{2}(x^2 + 4x)} = \frac{(x+3)(x+4)}{x(x+4)} = \frac{(x+3)\cancel{(x+4)}}{x\cancel{(x+4)}} = \frac{(x+3)}{x}$$

The final answer is $\frac{(x+3)}{x}$.

**QUESTION 2**

If $(x © y) = (4x^3 + 12 + 12y + 6y^2)$, then what expression is equivalent to $(4x) © 12$?

    A. $256x^3 + 1020$

    B. $1276$

    C. $64x^3 + 1020$

    D. $16x + 1020$

**Answer:** A

**Explanation:** To solve this problem, (4x) needs to be substituted for x in the expression $4x^3 + 12 + 12y + 6y^2$. In the same expression, 12 needs to be substituted for y. These substitutions result in:

$$4(4x)^3 + 12 + 12 \times 12 + 6 \times 12^2 = 4(4x)^3 + 12 + 144 + 6 \times 144 = 4(4x)^3 + 1020$$

It is necessary to evaluate the expression $(4x)^3$. This is equivalent to $(4x) \times (4x) \times (4x)$, which results in $64x^3$. Incorporating this value into the expression results in:

$$4(4x)^3 + 1020 = 4 \times 64x^3 + 1020 = 256x^3 + 1020$$

## QUESTION 3

The point A for the following graph represents what point?

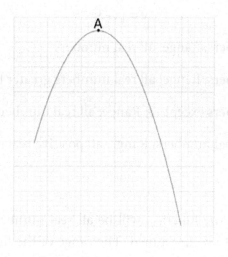

A. minimum

B. maximum

C. vertex

D. B and C

**Answer:** D

**Explanation:** The vertex of a parabola is the point where the parabola crosses its axis of symmetry. If the parabola is concave up, then the vertex will be the lowest point on the parabola, which would be the minimum. If the parabola is concave down, then the vertex will be the highest point on the parabola, which would be the maximum. In this graph, Point A is the vertex of a concave down parabola, so it is also the maximum.

**QUESTION 4**

What is the range and domain of the function shown below?

$$y = |x+3| - 5$$

A.  Domain: all real numbers; Range: all real numbers

B.  Domain: all real numbers; Range: all real numbers greater than -5

C.  Domain: all real numbers except -3; Range: all real numbers greater than -5

D.  Domain: all positive real numbers; Range: all positive real numbers

**Answer:** B

**Explanation:** The domain of the function will be all real numbers because there is no number that will cause the value of y to be undefined. The range of the function will be all real numbers greater than -5. -5 is the smallest term because the smallest number that will result from the absolute value is 0, and 0 − 5 = -5.

## QUESTION 5

In what intervals of the domain shown below does the graph increase?

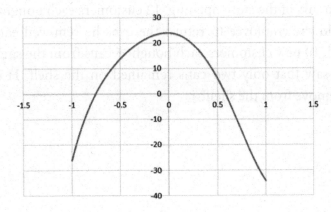

A. [0,1]

B. [-1,1]

C. [-0.75, 0.55]

D. [-1, 0]

**Answer:** D

**Explanation:** A function is increasing if the value of y is increasing as the value of x is increasing. This behavior is seen in the interval [-1, 0].

**QUESTION 6**

When the grocery store opens, a store manager tells an employee to take half of the cans off of a shelf. In the first four hours of the store opening, 12 customers each bought 3 cans from the shelf. The manager then told the employee to return the cans he removed earlier back to the shelf. Before the store closed, 10 new customers each bought 5 cans from the shelf. When the store was closing, the manager saw that only two cans remained on the shelf. How many cans did the employee originally remove from the shelf?

A. 88

B. 44

C. 25

D. 18

**Answer:** B

**Explanation:** To solve this problem, it is best to assign a variable to define the total number of cans originally on the shelf upon the store opening; this variable will be x. The employee removed $0.5x$ from the shelf before any customers bought the cans, so there was a total of $x - 0.5x$ cans available to be purchased. With these cans on the shelf, 12 customers each removed 3 cans, which totals to 36 cans removed. After these 36 cans have been removed, the employee returns the $0.5x$ cans that were initially removed. These two events can be added to the expression of the total cans available to purchase; the result is: $x - 0.5x - 36 + 0.5x$, which simplifies to $x - 36$. After the employee placed the cans back on the shelf, 10 customers each removed 5 cans from the shelf. This causes the number of cans on the shelf to decrease by 50, which can be expressed by $x - 36 - 50$. The manager sees that the total number of cans remaining on the shelf is 2, the expression of $x - 36 - 50$ can be set equal to 2. With this equation, the unknown variable can be solved; this results in a value of 88 for x. The question asks for the number of cans originally removed, which was equal to $0.5x$; this number is 44.

# QUESTION 7

What is the value of p in the figure below?

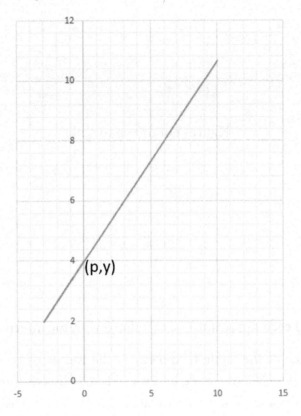

A. -4

B. 2/3

C. 0

D. 4

**Answer:** C

**Explanation:** Coordinate (p, y) is the y-intercept for the line shown. The letter p represents the x-coordinate of the y-intercept. By definition, the x-coordinate of the y-intercept is 0. Thus, the answer is A.

# QUESTION 8

Which of the following shapes has the largest area?

  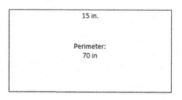 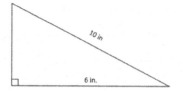

Figures not drawn to scale

A. Circle

B. Square

C. Rectangle

D. Triangle

**Answer:** C

**Explanation:** The area of each figure must be calculated with the information that is given.

The circumference of the circle is known, so the radius of the circle can be calculated. Dividing the known circumference by $2\pi$ yields a radius of 8 inches. The radius is then used to calculate the area. The area is calculated to be $64\pi \approx 201.06$ in.

The perimeter of the square is known, so the side of each square can be calculated. Dividing the known perimeter by 4 yields a side length of 12.5 inches. The side length is then used to calculate the area. The area is calculated to be 156.25 inches².

The perimeter and one side length of the rectangle is known, so the other side length can be calculated. To solve for the unknown side length, the first step is to multiply the known side length by 2 and subtract this product from the known perimeter. Then the result of this subtraction is divided by 2. These operations yield a side length of 20 inches $(70 - (15 \times 2) = 40; 40 \div 2 = 20)$. The two sides are then used to calculate the area of the figure. The area is calculated to be 300 inches².

The lengths of the hypotenuse and one side are known, so the other side length can be calculated via Pythagorean theorem. The Pythagorean theorem yields a side with length 8 inches ($\sqrt{10^2 - 6^2} = 8$). The side length calculated represents the height for the other side length, so these two side lengths can be used to calculate the area of the triangle. The area is calculated to be 24 inches².

From the above calculations, the rectangle is the largest area.

**QUESTION 9**

Angle P is 24 degrees more than Angle Q. Angle P can be represented with variable x, and Angle Q can be represented with variable y. If Angles P and Q are supplementary, then which of the following set of equation can be used to solve for x and y?

A.  $x + y = 90°$

   $2y + 24 = 90°$

B.  $x + y = 180°$

   $2y + 24 = 180°$

C.  $x + y = 180°$

   $2x + 24 = 180°$

D.  $x + y = 90°$

   $2x + 24 = 90°$

**Answer:** B

**Explanation:** Since Angles P and Q are supplementary, their sum is equal to 180 degrees. If Angle P is larger than Angle Q, which is taken to be y, by 24 degrees, then Angle P is equal to y + 24°. Taking the sum of Angle P (which is y) and Angle Q (which is y+24) gives 2y + 24°. This expression can be set equal to 180°. The second expression, which will help solve for the value of x, is x + y = 180°, which represents the sum of Angle P and Angle Q.

# QUESTION 10

Which of the following equations will be perpendicular to the following graph?

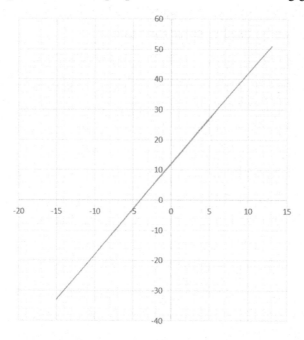

A. $y = 3x + 12$

B. $y = -\frac{1}{3}x + 9$

C. $y = \frac{1}{3}x + 12$

D. $y = \frac{1}{3}x - 12$

**Answer:** B

**Explanation:** The first approach to this problem is to find the linear equation that represents the graph shown. The graph makes it apparent that the y intercept is 12. The slope will be calculated by using the slope formula, which is shown below. Using the points (0, 12) and (6, 30), the slope is calculated to be $(\frac{30-12}{6-0}) = 3$. Taking into account the slope and y intercept, the equation of the line is $y = 3x + 12$.

The problem statement asks to identify an equation for a line that is perpendicular to $y = 3x + 12$. Perpendicular lines have a unique relationship in that the slopes of the two perpendicular lines have a product of -1. Perpendicular lines have negative, inverse slopes. If the slope of one line is 3, then a line perpendicular to it will have a slope of -1/3. The y intercepts of two perpendicular lines do not have any relationship, so they can have any value.

## QUESTION 11

In the figure below $\overleftrightarrow{AB} \parallel \overleftrightarrow{CD}$ and ∢EKA >∢GIA, which of the following statements is NOT true?

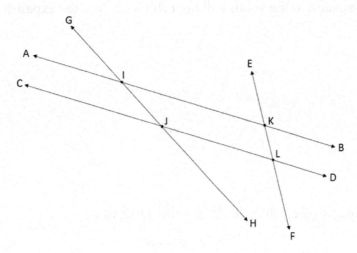

A.  ∢GIB >∢AKF

B.  ∢GJD = ∢ CJH

C.  ∢EKB + ∢AKF + ∢BKF + ∢EKA = 360°

D.  ∢EKB = ∢GJD

**Answer:** D

**Explanation:** The best approach to this problem is to evaluate each of the answer choices given.

The first answer choice states that angle GIB is larger than angle AKF. It is helpful to note that angle AKF is equivalent to angle EKB because they are vertical angles.  Angle EKB is the supplement to angle EKA and angle GIB is the supplement to angle GIA. Since angle GIA is known to be less than angle EKA, Angle GIB will be greater than angle EKB. Thus, answer choice A is true.

The second answer choice states that angle GJD is equivalent to angle CJH. This is true because those two angles are vertical angles.

In the third answer choice, angles EKB and EKA are supplementary and angles AKF and BKF are supplementary. Two pairs of supplementary angles will sum to 360 degrees.

The fourth answer choice states that angles EKB and GJD are equivalent. Angle EKB is equivalent to angle AKF because they are vertical angles. Angle GJD is equivalent to angle GIB because they are vertical angles. Answer choice A proved that angle GIB is greater than angle AKF, so the statement that these two are equivalent is not true.

## QUESTION 12

The radius of a right circular cylinder is increased by 200%. What is the ratio of the volume of the cylinder after the expansion to the volume of the cylinder before the expansion?

A. 0.5

B. 1.33

C. 2

D. 4

**Answer:** D

**Explanation:** The volume of a right cylinder is shown below.

$$\text{Volume} = \pi r^2 h$$

The questions asks for the ratio of the volume of the cylinder after the expansion to the volume of the cylinder before the expansion. This ratio is shown below.

$$\frac{\pi r_{after}^2 h}{\pi r_{before}^2 h}$$

Since the height, which does not change, and $\pi$ is present in both the numerator and denominator, those two cancel out. The simplified ratio is shown below.

$$\frac{r_{after}^2}{r_{before}^2}$$

Since the new radius is equal to two times the old radius, a substitution of $r_{after} = 2r_{before}$ can be made into the ratio. This substitution results in a value of 4, as shown below.

$$\frac{(2 \, r_{before})^2}{r_{before}^2} = \frac{4(r_{before})^2}{r_{before}^2} = 4$$

**QUESTION 13**

A student draws a perfect regular pentagon on a piece of paper using a ruler and a protractor. After drawing the polygon, the student measures the angle at one corner to be 105°. What is the percent error of this measurement?

    A.  2.78%

    B.  2.86%

    C.  3%

    D.  45.8%

**Answer:** A

**Explanation:** To answer this question, it needs to be noted that the student drew a perfect regular pentagon and that the only error was during the measurement process. It is known that a regular pentagon has 5 equal angles of 108°. Thus, a measurement of 105 represents a percent error of:

$$\frac{108\text{-}105}{108} \times 100 = 2.78\%$$

## QUESTION 14

A newly designed battery is shaped as rectangular prism with dimensions of 40.3 mm by 21.2 mm by 8.3 mm. If 10 of these batteries weigh 7.48 x 10³ mg, then what is the density of the newly designed battery in mg/mm³?

    A. 0.105

    B. 1.05

    C. 9.48

    D. 10.5

**Answer:** A

**Explanation:** Density is defined as mass divided by volume. The mass of a battery can be calculated by dividing the weight of 10 batteries by 10; this results in a weight of $\left(\frac{7.48 \times 10^3}{10}\right)=748$ mg per battery. The volume of the battery can be calculated by using the volume of the rectangular prism; this results in a volume of $40.3 \times 21.2 \times 8.3 = 7091.19$ mm³. The density can then be calculated by dividing the mass of one battery by the volume of one battery; this results in a density of 0.105 mg/mm³.

## QUESTION 15

Which of the following is NOT a continuous variable?

    A.  number of chairs in a classroom

    B.  temperature in a classroom

    C.  weight of the students in a classroom

    D.  height of the students in a classroom

**Answer:** A

**Explanation:** To solve this problem, the definitions of continuous and discrete variables need to be known.

- Continuous variable: a variable that can take any value between two measurements or numbers.
- Discrete variable: a variable that takes only values from a countable set of numbers (0, 1, 2, 3, …)

In the answer choices given, height, weight, and temperature can take any value. For example, a student can have a height of 60.2145898 inches, a student can weigh 120.25478 pounds, or the temperature can be 68.987 F°. However, the number of chairs cannot take any value. Its value must be a countable, natural number. For example, the number of chairs can be 2, 5, or 8, but not 2.14. Thus, the number of chairs in a classroom is not a continuous variable.

## QUESTION 16

Which of the following is true if $\overleftrightarrow{AB}\parallel\overleftrightarrow{CD}$, $\overleftrightarrow{EF}\parallel\overleftrightarrow{GH}$, $\overrightarrow{KI}$ bisects $\angle AKF$, and $\overrightarrow{JL}$ bisects $\angle ALH$?

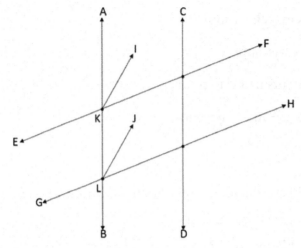

A. $\angle AKI + \angle IKF = \angle GLB$

B. $\angle AKI > \angle IKF$

C. $\angle AKE = \angle AKF$

D. $\angle EKB = \angle AKI$

**Answer:** A

**Explanation:** The best approach to this problem is to evaluate each answer choice. Answer choice A states that the sum of angles AKI and IKF equals the angle GLB. The sum of angles AKI and IKF equals angle AKF, because $\overrightarrow{KI}$ bisects $\angle AKF$. The two angles that result from the bisection are equal and add up to the larger angle that was broken into two, which was $\angle AKF$. Angle AKF is equal to angle GLB because they are congruent alternate exterior angles. Option A is a true statement.

## QUESTION 17

There are 20 people participated in a clinical research trial for a new pill that claims to help people lose weight. Every week, the lab assistants record the weights of the 20 people. The data below shows the weight loss for the 20 people after 10 weeks of the research trial. What is the mode, mean, median, and range for the data set?

| Stem | Leaf |
|------|------|
| 0 | 6 8 8 9 |
| 1 | 1 2 4 5 5 8 8 8 |
| 2 | 0 1 1 5 6 8 9 |
| 3 | 0 |

A. Mode = 18, Mean = 17.6, Median = 18, Range = 24

B. Mode = 8, Mean = 5.1, Median = 8, Range = 9

C. Mode = 1, Mean = 1.5, Median = 1.5, Range = 3

D. Mode = 10, Mean = 15, Median = 15, Range = 30

**Answer:** A

**Explanation:** The data is presented in a stem-and-leaf plot. To read the data, each digit in the leaf section of the plot is placed after the last digit shown in the stem section. For example, in the second row of the data set, the actual values are 11, 12, 13, 15, 15, 18, 18, and 18. The same analysis can be performed for the other rows of the data set.

The mode of the data set will be the most occurring data value. This value is 18.

The mean of the data set will be the average of all the data values. This is calculated by taking the sum of all values (352) and dividing it by the total number of values (20). The result is 17.6.

The median of the data set is the middle number in the data set. This is determined by placing the data values in order from least to greatest or greatest to least. If there are an odd number of data values in the data set, then the median will be middle number. If there an even number of data values in the data set, then the median will be mean of the two central numbers. In this data set, there are an even number of data values, so the mean of the two central numbers is 18.

The range of the data set is the difference between the largest and smallest data values. In this data set, the largest value is 30 and the smallest value is 6, so the range is 24.

## QUESTION 18

The perimeter of a heptagon is 180 and the lengths of the sides are in the ratio 1:3:5:7:8:9:12. What is the measure of the longest side of the heptagon?

   A. 4

   B. 25.7

   C. 48

   D. 45

**Answer:** C

**Explanation:** The lengths are given in ratio form. To solve for any of the lengths, it is necessary to develop an equation that takes into account the proportionality among the side lengths. This can be done with the following equation:

$$1x + 3x + 5x + 7x + 8x + 9x + 12x = 180$$

Solve the equation for x yields result of 4. Using this value of x, it becomes obvious that the longest side of the heptagon has a length of 48.

## QUESTION 19

The following figure shows a hexagonal prism separated into its 8 faces. If the height of the rectangles is 24 cm and the width of the rectangles is 8 cm, then what is the total surface area of the hexagonal prism?

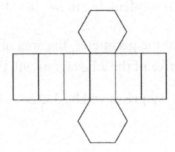

A. 1484.56 cm$^2$

B. 1152 cm$^2$

C. 358.28 cm$^2$

D. 332.56 cm$^2$

**Answer:** A

**Explanation:** To solve for the total surface area of the hexagonal prism, the areas of the 6 rectangles and 2 hexagons needs to be calculated.

The area of one rectangle is 192 cm$^2$. The total area of the 6 rectangles is 1152 cm$^2$.

The area of the regular hexagon can be calculated with the formula shown below.

$$\text{Area of Regular Polygon} = \frac{1}{2} \times p \times a$$

The variable p is the perimeter of the hexagon. The perimeter of the hexagon is 48 cm. The variable a is the apothem of regular hexagon. The apothem is the distance from the midpoint of the polygon to the midpoint of a side of the polygon. For this hexagon, the apothem is not given. Rather a distance from the midpoint to a vertex of the hexagon is given. The apothem can be calculated by performing the Pythagorean Theorem on the triangle shown below.

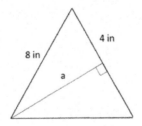

Since the apothem is a perpendicular bisector, there is enough information to calculate the apothem of the regular hexagon. Since the apothem is a perpendicular bisector, it creates a right triangle, as shown in the figure above. The hypotenuse of this right triangle is the radius of the circle. The base is half of the side length (4 cm), and the height is the apothem. Using the Pythagorean Theorem, the apothem is calculated to be $\sqrt{8^2 - 4^2} = 6.93$cm.

Using the value of the apothem and the perimeter, the area of the hexagon is calculated to be 0.5 $\times$ 48 $\times$ 6.93=166.28 cm$^2$. The total area of the 2 hexagons will then be 166.28 $\times$ 2=332.56 cm$^2$.

The total surface area of the hexagonal prism will be 332.56 + 1152=1484.56 cm$^2$.

## QUESTION 20

A mother was looking for a daycare in her city to send her child. She came across 50 different daycares, each with a different hourly cost. The following histogram summarizes the costs of the daycares. Which of the following statements regarding the mean, mode, and median are true?

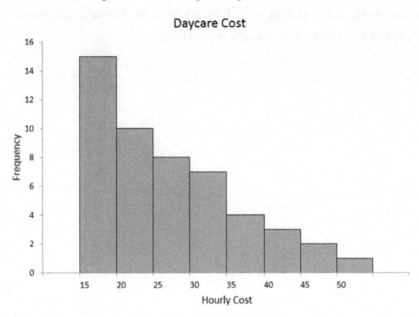

A. Mode < Median < Mean

B. Mean = Mode = Median

C. Mean < Median < Mode

D. Not enough information given

**Answer:** A

**Explanation:** To solve this problem, certain properties of right skewed and left skewed distributions need to be known.

In a right skewed distribution, majority of the data values cluster at the lower end of the distribution. The peaks of the histogram will be larger at the left end and decrease in size as the class limits increase. In a right skewed distribution, majority of the data values fall to the left of the mean, so the mode and median will be less than the mean; the mode will be less than the median. These descriptions prove that option A is the correct answer because the graph given shows a right skewed distribution

In a left skewed distribution, majority of the data values cluster at the higher end of the distribution. The peaks of the histogram will be larger at the right end and decrease in size as the class limits decrease. In a left skewed distribution, majority of the data values fall to the right of the mean, so the mode and median will be greater than the mean; the mode will be larger than the median. These descriptions correspond to option C, which is not a correct answer for this problem.

If unimodal, symmetric distribution, the data values are evenly distributed on both sides of the mean, so the mean, mode, and median will all be equivalent. These descriptions correspond to option B, which is not a correct answer for this problem.

# QUESTION 21

Mrs. Garcia asked her students how many hours they slept every school night. She then took this data and compared it with the grades those students earned on their first exam. The two separate sets of data are shown below. Which of the following scatter plots best models the data sets?

| Student | Exam Score | Student | Exam Score | Student | Exam Score | Student | Exam Score | Student | Exam Score |
|---------|-----------|---------|-----------|---------|-----------|---------|-----------|---------|-----------|
| 1 | 55 | 6 | 78 | 11 | 85 | 16 | 89 | 21 | 97 |
| 2 | 58 | 7 | 78 | 12 | 85 | 17 | 91 | 22 | 98 |
| 3 | 62 | 8 | 79 | 13 | 87 | 18 | 95 | 23 | 99 |
| 4 | 74 | 9 | 79 | 14 | 88 | 19 | 95 | 24 | 100 |
| 5 | 75 | 10 | 84 | 15 | 89 | 20 | 96 | 25 | 100 |

| Student | Hours of Sleep | Student | Hours of Sleep | Student | Hours of Sleep | Student | Hours of Sleep | Student | Hours of Sleep |
|---------|----------------|---------|----------------|---------|----------------|---------|----------------|---------|----------------|
| 1 | 12 | 6 | 8 | 11 | 8 | 16 | 8.5 | 21 | 8 |
| 2 | 2 | 7 | 8 | 12 | 8.5 | 17 | 8 | 22 | 7.5 |
| 3 | 10 | 8 | 9 | 13 | 9 | 18 | 7.5 | 23 | 8 |
| 4 | 5 | 9 | 8.5 | 14 | 9 | 19 | 10 | 24 | 7.5 |
| 5 | 5 | 10 | 7.5 | 15 | 9.5 | 20 | 8.5 | 25 | 6 |

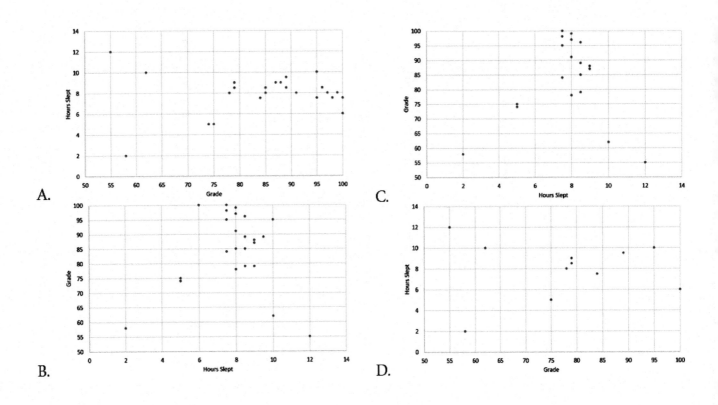

A.

B.

C.

D.

**Answer:** B

**Explanation:** The correct answer to this problem requires understanding which of the two values will be the dependent and independent variable. The independent variable will be the hours slept because this does not depend on the grade received on the exam. The numerical grade received on the exam will depend on the hours slept, so the grade will be the dependent variable. The dependent variable is plotted on the vertical axis and the independent variable on the horizontal axis. This eliminates answer choices A and D. Answer choice C is eliminated because it does not plot all the information. The correct answer choice is B.

## QUESTION 22

A high school club plans to sell chocolate chip cookies for a fundraising event. The club has $125 to invest in ingredients. One box contains 20 ounces of cookie dough and costs $20, and one package of chocolate chips costs $3. If x ounces of cookie dough and y packages of chocolate chips are needed, which of the following inequalities can be used to model the possible number of ounces of cookie dough and chocolate chips packages that can be bought?

    A.  $20x+3y \geq 125$

    B.  $20x+3y \leq 125$

    C.  $\frac{20}{x}+\frac{3}{y}>125$

    D.  $\frac{20}{x}-\frac{3}{y}>125$

**Answer:** B

**Explanation:** The cost of the possible number of ounces of cookie dough and packages of chocolate chips must not exceed the total amount of money, which is $125. Therefore, the "less than or equal" symbol, $\leq$, is the most appropriate. The "20x" is obtained from the question as one box of cookie dough cost $20, and the expression "3y" is obtained from the statement "one package of chocolate chips costs $3".

## QUESTION 23

If $-\frac{4}{5} < 2t+5 < \frac{5}{2}$, what is one possible value of $6t+15$?

    A.  -4

    B.  -3

    C.  6

    D.  8

**Answer:** C

**Explanation:** Multiply all parts of the inequality by 3.

$$-\frac{4}{5} < 2t+5 < \frac{5}{2}$$

$$-\frac{12}{5} < 6t+15 < \frac{15}{2}$$

Of the answer choices, 6 is the only number between $-\frac{12}{5}$ and $\frac{15}{2}$.

# QUESTION 24

In a laboratory experiment, the population of mice M doubles every 15 days. It is reported that the experiment starts out with 20 mice. Assuming no mice die during the experiment, which of the following equations represents the number of mice after d days?

A. $20+2^{\frac{d}{15}}$

B. $20+2^d$

C. $2(20)^{\frac{d}{15}}$

D. $20(2)^{\frac{d}{15}}$

**Answer:** D

**Explanation:** The best way to answer this question is to create a table on the population of mice increasing every day.

| Days | Population of Mice |
|------|--------------------|
| 0    | 20                 |
| 15   | 40                 |
| 30   | 80                 |
| 45   | 160                |
| 60   | 320                |

With the information in the table, one can test each answer choice and match the information. Option D is the correct answer that matches the results in the table.

**QUESTION 25**

If the $\frac{6x^2}{3x+1}$ is written in form $\frac{1}{3x+1}$ +A, what is A in terms of x?

    A.  $2x-\frac{2}{3}$

    B.  3x-1

    C.  $2x^2-1$

    D.  $6x^2-1$

**Answer:** B

**Explanation:** Perform the long division of polynomials $\frac{6x^2}{3x+1}$.

$$
\begin{array}{r}
2x \quad - \quad \frac{2}{3} \\
\hline
3x+1 \,\big|\, 6x^2 \qquad\qquad \\
6x^2 + 2x \\
\hline
-\,2x \\
-\,2x - \frac{2}{3} \\
\hline
\frac{2}{3}
\end{array}
$$

The result is $2x-\frac{2}{3}+\frac{\frac{2}{3}}{3x+1}$. This can be written in the desired format $\frac{1}{3x+1}$ +A by multiplying the entire expression by $\frac{3}{2}$.

$$2x-\frac{2}{3}+\frac{2}{3(3x+1)}=\frac{3}{2}\left(2x-\frac{2}{3}+\frac{2}{3(3x+1)}\right)=3x-1+\frac{1}{3x+1}$$

Clearly, B is equivalent to 3x-1.

# QUESTION 26

A car rental company charges $10.00 per day plus tax for a basic automobile. The tax rate is 8.25%, and the company also charges a one-time untaxed fee of $75.00. If a person rents a basic automobile for x days and spends $120 dollars in gas, which of the following represents the amount of money spent by this person?

    A.  1.0825(10.00x)+195

    B.  (10.00+8.25x)+195

    C.  1.0825(10.00x+195)

    D.  8.25(10.00x)+195

**Answer:** A

**Explanation:** $10.00 is charged during x days, and this amount is taxed at a rate of 8.25%. This translates into 1.0825(10.00x). The untaxed fee of $75.00 and the amount spent in gas of $120.00 add to a total of $195. Combining 1.0825(10.00x) and $195, gives the expression 1.0825(10.00x)+195.

## QUESTION 27

$$\frac{1-\frac{1}{\sqrt{3}}}{1+\frac{1}{\sqrt{3}}}$$

What is the expression above equivalent to?

A. $1+\sqrt{3}$

B. $2-\sqrt{3}$

C. $1+2\sqrt{3}$

D. $\frac{2}{3}$

**Answer:** B

**Explanation:** First, multiply by the conjugate to get rid of the square root in the denominator.

$$\frac{1-\frac{1}{\sqrt{3}}}{1+\frac{1}{\sqrt{3}}} \times \frac{1-\frac{1}{\sqrt{3}}}{1-\frac{1}{\sqrt{3}}} = \frac{1-\frac{1}{\sqrt{3}}-\frac{1}{\sqrt{3}}+\left(\frac{1}{\sqrt{3}}\right)^2}{1-\frac{1}{\sqrt{3}}+\frac{1}{\sqrt{3}}-\left(\frac{1}{\sqrt{3}}\right)^2}$$

Second, combine like terms.

$$\frac{1-\frac{2}{\sqrt{3}}+\frac{1}{3}}{1-\frac{1}{3}} = \frac{\frac{4}{3}-\frac{2}{\sqrt{3}}}{\frac{2}{3}}$$

Third, avoid having a square root in the denominator by performing

$$\frac{2}{\sqrt{3}} \times \frac{\sqrt{3}}{\sqrt{3}} = \frac{2\sqrt{3}}{3}.$$

Fourth, the solution is found.

$$\frac{\frac{4}{3}-\frac{2\sqrt{3}}{3}}{\frac{2}{3}} = \frac{\frac{4}{3}}{\frac{2}{3}} - \frac{\frac{2\sqrt{3}}{3}}{\frac{2}{3}} = 2-\sqrt{3}$$

# QUESTION 28

A marketing company conducted a survey to determine the preference of different chips among five different age groups. The table below displays a summary of the survey results.

| Age Group (years old) | Preference | | |
| --- | --- | --- | --- |
| | Potato Chips | Corn Chips | Plantain Chips |
| 10-19 | 32 | 13 | 15 |
| 20-29 | 18 | 16 | 16 |
| 30-39 | 12 | 22 | 16 |
| 40-49 | 10 | 13 | 17 |
| 50-59 | 11 | 15 | 24 |
| Total | 83 | 79 | 88 |

According to the table, for which age group did the greatest percentage of people report they prefer corn chips?

    A.  20-29 years old

    B.  30-39 years old

    C.  40-49 years old

    D.  50-59 years old

**Answer:** B

**Explanation:** From the table, observe the column about corn chips. The age group of people 30-39 years old has the greater number of people, thus the greatest percentage.

## QUESTION 29

A kid plans to sell cups of lemonade in order to raise money for a birthday present. He has determined the cost for n cups of lemonade is modeled by the equation c=0.5n+18. Each cup of lemonade sells for $2, and the kid makes a profit when the money collected from the amount of cups sold exceeds the cost. Which of the following inequalities gives all possible values of n for which the kid will make a profit?

    A. n<12

    B. n>12

    C. n<18

    D. n>18

**Answer:** B

**Explanation:** It is provided that the kid makes a profit when the amount of money in sales is greater than the cost. This can be set up as a inequality comparing the money in sales with costs.

$$\text{money in sales} > \text{cost}$$

$$2n > 0.5n + 18$$

Solve for the amount of cups n.

$$2n - 0.5n > 18$$

$$1.5n > 18$$

$$n > \frac{18}{1.5}$$

$$n > 12$$

**QUESTION 30**

A fuel tank is one-quarter full when it has 6 gallons. After adding $20 worth of fuel, the tank is two-thirds full. In addition, the fuel price in dollars is $3.20 per gallon. If the car runs at 25 miles per gallon when going at an average speed of 50 miles/hour, which of the following functions, f, models the number of gallons of gas remaining in the tank t hours?

A. $f(t)=16-\frac{50}{25}t$

B. $f(t)=24-\frac{25}{50}t$

C. $f(t)=\frac{16-50t}{25}$

D. $f(t)=\frac{24-25t}{50}$

**Answer:** A

**Explanation:** It is necessary to find the number of gallons remaining after t hours of driving. Function can be described as

function of time=initial amount gallons in tank-gallons spent each hour

First, determine the total capacity of the tank. If 6 gallons is equivalent to one-quarter of the tank, then the full tank holds 24 gallons.

Second, determine the two-thirds of the full tank, which is the initial amount of gallons. It is $24\times\frac{2}{3}=16$ gallons.

Third, calculate the amount of gallons per hour. To get this, take the average speed and divide by the miles per gallon.

$$\frac{\text{average speed}}{\text{miles per gallon}}=\frac{50\frac{\text{miles}}{\text{hr}}}{25\frac{\text{miles}}{\text{gallon}}}=\frac{50}{25}\left(\frac{\text{gallons}}{\text{hr}}\right)$$

Subtracting gallons spent each hour from initial amount of gallons in the tank, the function is shown below.

$$f(t)=16-\frac{50}{25}t$$

## QUESTION 31

According to an article in a financial magazine, a company had an income of 3.6 billion dollars during the previous year. Based on this report, Kirk estimates that the company earned an average of 3 million dollars per month. Which of the following statements best describes Kirk's estimate for the company's average monthly income?

    A. The estimate is low by a factor of 10.

    B. The estimate is high by a factor of 10.

    C. The estimate is low by a factor of 100.

    D. The estimate is high by a factor of 100.

**Answer:** C

**Explanation:** One billion is equivalent to $1 \times 10^9$. Therefore 3.6 billion is equivalent to

$$3.6 \text{ billion} \left( \frac{1 \times 10^9}{1 \text{ billion}} \right) = 3.6 \times 10^9 = 3{,}600{,}000{,}000.$$

Divide such number by 12 to find the monthly average.

$$\frac{3{,}600{,}000{,}000}{12} = 300{,}000{,}000$$

Comparing to the 3 million estimated by the person reading the article, the estimate is low by a factor of 100.

**QUESTION 32**

$$24x=9y-15-3x$$

What is the x-intercept of the equation above?

A.  $-\dfrac{5}{9}$

B.  $-\dfrac{3}{8}$

C.  $\dfrac{1}{3}$

D.  $\dfrac{5}{8}$

**Answer:** A

**Explanation:** The x-intercept occurs when y=0. Therefore, plug in y=0 and solve for x.

$$24x=9y-15-3x$$

$$24x=9(0)-15-3x$$

$$24x=-15-3x$$

$$27x=-15$$

$$x=-\frac{15}{27}$$

$$x=-\frac{5}{9}$$

## QUESTION 33

Which of the following describes the graph of $y = \frac{1}{3}f(x)$ in the interval $0 \leq x \leq \infty$ if $f(x) = x^2$?

A. increases more rapidly

B. increases more slowly

C. decreases more rapidly

D. decreases more slowly

**Answer:** B

**Explanation:** The function $f(x) = x^2$ becomes wider when multiplied by $\frac{1}{3}$. Using the calculator, one can observe this by comparing the graphs of $f(x) = x^2$ and $y = \frac{1}{3}x^2$. In the function $y = \frac{1}{3}x^2$, the graph increases slowly as it goes upwards.

## QUESTION 34

A store sells toy cars for $4 and toy trucks for $6. The day before New Year's Day, the store sold 10 more cars than trucks and earns $260. Which system of equations could be used to find the number of cars C and trucks T that the store sold that day?

    A. $C+T=10$ and $4C+6T=260$

    B. $C-T=10$ and $4C+6T=260$

    C. $C+10T=260$ and $4C-6T=0$

    D. $10C-T=0$ and $4C-6T=100$

**Answer:** B

**Explanation:** C and T are cars and trucks, respectively. The statement indicates that the store sold 10 more cars than trucks. It becomes $C=T+10$. Additionally, the store also earns $260 which translates into $4C+6T=260$. These two equations form a system that can be used to find the number of cars and trucks.

## QUESTION 35

What is the area of the shaded region? (The hexagon shown is a regular hexagon)

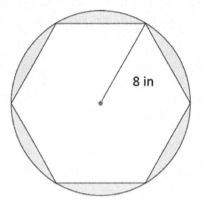

A. 201.06 inches

B. 166.28 inches

C. 34.79 inches

D. 9.06 inches

**Answer:** C

**Explanation:** The area of the shaded region is the result of subtracting the area of the regular hexagon from the area of the circle. The area of the circle is $\pi \times 8^2 = 64\pi$. The area of the regular hexagon can be calculated with the formula shown below.

$$\text{Area of Regular Polygon} = \frac{1}{2} \times p \times a$$

The variable p is the perimeter of the hexagon. The perimeter of the hexagon inscribed in the circle is 8×6 = 48. The variable a is the apothem of regular hexagon. The apothem is the distance from the midpoint of the polygon to the midpoint of a side of the polygon. For this hexagon, the apothem is not given. Rather a distance from the midpoint to a vertex of the hexagon is given. The apothem can be calculated by performing Pythagorean theorem on the triangle shown below.

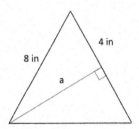

Since the apothem is a perpendicular bisector, there is enough information to calculate the apothem of the regular hexagon. Since the apothem is a perpendicular bisector, it creates a right triangle, as shown in the figure above. The hypotenuse of this right triangle is the radius of the circle. The base is half of the side length (4 in), and the height is the apothem. Using the Pythagorean Theorem, the apothem is calculated to be $\sqrt{8^2 - 4^2} = 6.93$.

Using the value of the apothem and the perimeter, the area of the hexagon is calculated to be 0.5 × 48 × 6.93=166.28. This area is subtracted from the area of the circle, and this results in 34.79 inches.

# QUESTION 36

An aerial view of segment of drill pipe is shown below. The outer diameter of the drill pipe is 22.5 inches. The area of the shaded portion is 83.5 in² . What is the inner diameter of the drill pipe? (The inner diameter is labeled as ID in the figure below)

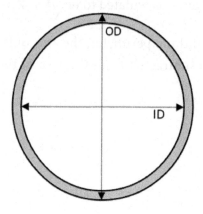

A. 10 in

B. 13.13 in

C. 20 in

D. 21.9 in

**Answer:** C

**Explanation:** The shaded portion exists because the area of the larger circle (of diameter OD) was reduced by the area of the smaller circle (of diameter ID). To obtain the inner diameter, an equation needs to be set up with the ID as the unknown variable. This equation is show below:

$$\text{shaded area} = \pi \times \left( \left( \frac{22.5}{2} \right)^2 - \left( \frac{ID}{2} \right)^2 \right)$$

Since the shaded area is known to be 83.5 in², the above formula can be solved for ID. The result is 20 inches.

**QUESTION 37**

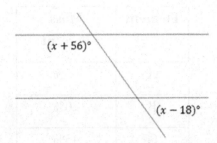

In the figure above, there are two parallel horizontal lines crossed by slanted line. What is the value of x?

    A.  67

    B.  68

    C.  70

    D.  71

**Answer:** D

**Explanation:** The angles shown in the figure can be rearranged as in the figure below.

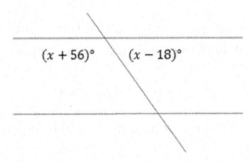

The sum of those two angles makes 180°, which allows writing the equation:

$$(x+56)+(x-18)=180.$$

Solve for x to find the solution.

$$2x+38=180$$
$$2x=142$$
$$x=71$$

**QUESTION 38**

| Element | Mass Percent |
|---------|--------------|
| A | 35% |
| B | 20% |
| C | 45% |

The table above shows the percent composition of mass of the elements in a chemical compound. If element A weighs 14 grams by itself, what is the weight of the element C in grams?

    A. 10

    B. 16

    C. 18

    D. 40

**Answer:** C

**Explanation:** The first step in this question is to divide the weight of element A by its mass percent in decimal form to obtain the weight of the entire compound.

$$\frac{14 \text{ grams}}{0.35} = 40.0 \text{ grams}$$

After this, the weight of the entire compound is multiplied by the mass percentage of element C to find its weight.

$$40.0 \text{ grams} \times 0.45 = 18 \text{ grams}$$

**QUESTION 39**

The minute hand of a clock makes one quarter of a circumference as 15 minutes pass. What angle, in degrees, does the hour hand move?

    A. 7.5

    B. 15.0

    C. 28.0

    D. 30.0

**Answer:** A

**Explanation:** Consider a regular clock. As the minute hand completes a revolution, the hour hand moves 1 hour. A quarter of a circumference is 90° which is 15 minutes in the minute hand of a clock. This indicates that the hour hand would move one quarter of the distance between two hour marks. Each division of the hours is 30°, since 360° is divided by 12 equal areas. By inspection, the angle that the hour hand makes in 15 minutes is 30°/4=7.5°.

**QUESTION 40**

There are four consecutive numbers. The last number is equal to the sum of half of the first number, one-third of the second number, and one-fourth of the third number. What is the first number?

    A.  22

    B.  23

    C.  25

    D.  26

**Answer:** D

**Explanation:** Start by giving a value of x to the first number. Then, the statement "The last number is equal to the sum of half of the first number, one-third of the second number, and one-fourth of the third number" can be put into an equation as

$$x+3=\frac{x}{2}+\frac{x+1}{3}+\frac{x+2}{4}$$

Simply solve for x to obtain the answer.

$$x+3=\frac{x}{2}+\frac{x}{3}+\frac{1}{3}+\frac{x}{4}+\frac{2}{4}$$

$$x-\frac{x}{2}-\frac{x}{3}-\frac{x}{4}=\frac{1}{3}+\frac{1}{2}-3$$

$$-\frac{1}{12}x=-\frac{13}{6}$$

$$x=26$$

**QUESTION 41**

Select all the appropriate zeros for the function $x^3 - 6x^2 + 11x - 6$.

$$3 \quad 2 \quad 1 \quad -1 \quad 2 \quad 0 \quad 3$$

**Answer:** 3, 2, 1

**Explanation:** The zeros of a function are the x coordinate values when a function equals 0. To determine the zeros, the expression $x^3 - 6x^2 + 11x - 6$ is set equal to 0 and solved for x. This results in a values of 3, 2, and 1 for x.

**QUESTION 42**

Which of the following options can be solutions to the inequality: $|3x + 9| < 5x + 7$?

$$-3 \quad -5 \quad 1 \quad 3 \quad 5$$

**Answer:** 3, 5

**Explanation:** To solve an inequality of the form $|x| < a$, the absolute value signs are removed and the following inequality is solved: $-a < x < a$. The left portion is solved: $-a < x$. The right portion is solved as $x < a$.

$|3x + 9| < 5x + 7$ becomes $-5x - 7 < 3x + 9 < 5x + 7$

$-5x - 7 < 3x + 9$ becomes $-5x - 3x - 7 + 7 < 3x - 3x + 9 + 7$ which is equivalent to $-8x < 16$. This results in $x > -2$.

$3x + 9 < 5x + 7$ becomes $3x - 3x + 9 - 7 < 5x - 3x + 7 - 7$ which is equivalent to $2 < 2x$. This results in $1 < x$.

The answer to the inequality becomes x>1, so any number greater than 1 is a solution to the inequality.

## QUESTION 43

Which of the following numbers can be the length of the third side of a triangle, whose other two sides are 10 and 14?

$$3 \qquad 5 \qquad 12 \qquad 18 \qquad 25$$

**Answer:** 5, 12, 18

**Explanation:** If 10 and 14 are to be taken as the lengths of two sides of a triangle, then the third side length must be between 4 (difference between 14 and 10) and 24 (sum of 14 and 10).

## QUESTION 44

If a triangle has a known angle of 32, which of the following pairs of numbers can be the measurements of the two other angles?

$$52 \text{ and } 96 \qquad 90 \text{ and } 45 \qquad 79 \text{ and } 116 \qquad 45 \text{ and } 60 \qquad 116 \text{ and } 32$$

**Answer:** 52 and 96; 116 and 32

**Explanation:** The sum of all three angles of a triangle is 180. If one angle has a measurement of 32, then the two other angles must have a total measurement of 148, which include the pairs 52 and 96; 116 and 32.

## QUESTION 45

Which of the following numbers are considered real numbers?

$$0.75 \qquad 0 \qquad 10 \qquad -28 \qquad \sqrt{-2}, \qquad \sqrt{-25}$$

**Answer:** 0.75, 0, 10, - 28

**Explanation:** Square roots of negative numbers are not defined for real numbers.

## QUESTION 46

Five friends go to a donut shop. John orders 6 donuts. Mary orders 150% more donuts than John. Carol orders 3 more donuts than Mary. Hector orders 25% of the donuts Carol orders. Eric orders 2 more donuts than Hector. Which of the following people ordered more than 5 donuts?

John   Mary   Carol   Hector Eric

**Answer:** John, Mary, and Carol

**Explanation:** The best approach is to determine the number of donuts each of the five people have order.

> John orders 6 donuts.
>
> Mary orders 150% more donuts than John, so she orders 6 × 1.50=9.
>
> Carol orders 3 more donuts than Mary, so she order 9+3=12.
>
> Hector orders 25% of the donuts Carol orders, so he orders 3 donuts.
>
> Eric orders 2 more donuts than Hector, so he orders 5 donuts.

Of the five people, only John, Mary and Carol have ordered more than 5 donuts.

## QUESTION 47

Which of the following numbers is greater than 125 but less than 875?

A. -126

B. $1.25 \times 10^2$

C. $\frac{875}{10}$

D. $125 \times \sqrt{2}$

**Answer:** D

**Explanation:** Answer choice A is not greater than 125 because it is a negative number. Answer choice B is in scientific notation, and once expanded, its value is 125. 125 is equal to 125 and not greater than 125, so it is not the correct answer. Answer choice C is a fraction, and once expanded, its value is 87.5, which is not greater than 125. Answer choice D is the correct answer. Noticing that the square root of 2 is a value of 1.414, which is greater than 1 and less than 2. The value of answer choice D will be greater than 125 and less than 875, which fits within the range required for the question statement.

## QUESTION 48

If the multiplicative inverse of 1/5 is divided by the additive inverse of -5, what is the result?

    A.  0

    B.  1

    C.  -1

    D.  25

**Answer:** B

**Explanation:** To solve this problem, it is necessary to know the definitions of multiplicative and additive inverse.

The additive inverse of a number X is the number that needs to be added to X to achieve a sum of 0. The additive inverse of -5 is 5.

The multiplicative inverse of a number X is the number would result in a value of 1 when multiplied with X. The multiplicative inverse of 1/5 is 5.

The multiplicative inverse of 1/5, which is 5, divided by the additive inverse of -5, which is 5, will result in a value of 1.

**QUESTION 49**

What is the greatest common factor of 36 and 54?

    A. 1944

    B. 108

    C. 18

    D. 9

**Answer:** C

**Explanation:** To approach this problem, it is best to list the factors of both 36 and 54, which has been done below:

$$36: 1\ 2\ 3\ 4\ 6\ 9\ 12\ 18\ 36$$

$$54: 1\ 2\ 3\ 6\ 9\ 18\ 27\ 54$$

It becomes obvious that the greatest common factor of the two numbers is 18.

**QUESTION 50**

$$x^2+y^2+4x-10y=7$$

The equation of a circle in the xy-plane is shown above. What is the diameter of the circle?

**Answer:** $6\sqrt{3}$.

**Explanation:** Use the method of completing the square to write the equation of the circle in standard form
$(x-h)^2+(y-k)^2 = r^2$, where the center is located at (h,k) and r is the radius.

$$x^2+y^2-4x+8y=7$$

$$x^2-4x+\underline{\quad}+y^2+8y+\underline{\quad}=7$$

$$x^2-4x+4+y^2+8y+16=7+4+16$$

$$(x-2)^2+(y+4)^2=27$$

The radius is calculated from $r^2=27=9\times3=\sqrt{9}\times\sqrt{3}=3\sqrt{3}$. As a result, to obtain the diameter multiply by 2, which gives the answer of $6\sqrt{3}$.

## QUESTION 51

The function f is defined by $f(x)=x^3-x^2-14x+c$, where c is a constant. In the xy-plane, the graph of f intersects the x-axis at the three points (2,0), (3,0) and (p,0). What is the value of c?

A. -4

B. 12

C. 24

D. 32

**Answer:** C

**Explanation:** The intersections of the x-axis at (2,0), (3,0) and (p,0) can be used to write the function in terms of factors.

$$f(x)=(x-2)(x-3)(x+p)$$

This is equivalent to the given function. Set them equal to each other.

$$(x-2)(x-3)(x+p)=x^3-x^2-14x+c$$

Expand the polynomial on the left hand side.

$$(x^2-5x+6)(x+p)=x^3-x^2-14x+c$$

$$x^3+px^2-5x^2-5px+6x+6p=x^3-x^2-14x+c$$

Combine like-terms.

$$x^3+(p-5)x^2+(6-5p)x+6p=x^3-x^2-14x+c$$

Compare terms on both sides of the equation to find the value p, and then the value of c. First, compare the terms with $x^2$.

$$p-5=-1$$

$$p=4$$

Second, compare the terms with no variables and use the value of p just found.

$$6p=c$$

$$c=6(4)=24$$

## QUESTION 52

Which of the following could be the graph of y=2x-3?

A.

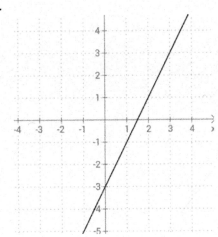

C.

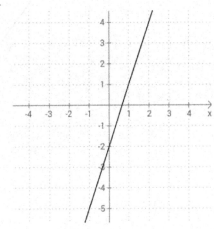

B.

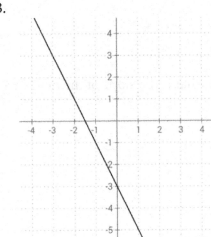

D.

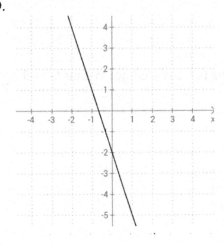

**Answer:** A

**Explanation:** The equation y=2x-3 is in form y=mx+b, where m is the slope and b is the y-intercept. The slope is positive, thus function increases as x increases. Moreover, the y-intercept is at y=-3. The only option that matches the description is option A.

**QUESTION 53**

A line is graphed in the xy-plane below.

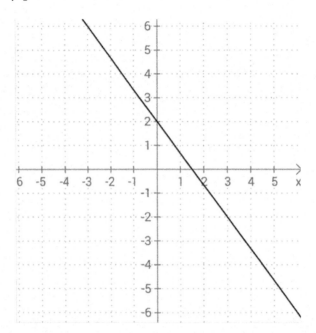

If the line is translated down 2 units and right 8 units, then what is the slope of the new line?

    A.  -4

    B.  $-\frac{4}{3}$

    C.  $-\frac{1}{4}$

    D.  $\frac{1}{4}$

**Answer:** B

**Explanation:** The translation of the line does not change the slope of the line. Therefore, the slope of the new line is the same as the slope of the original line.

Calculate the slope of the original line. It can be observed the line decreases 4 units in the vertical axis, while it increases 3 units in the horizontal axis.

$$\text{slope} = -\frac{4}{3}$$

## QUESTION 54

The elevation h in feet as a function of time of a group of hikers as they hike in a mountain is described by h=736t+3210. The variable t is time in hours, and the function is valid when 0<t<3. Which of the following statements is the best interpretation of the number 736 in the context of this problem?

 A. The elevation of the group during the first three hours of their hike.

 B. The elevation of the group as a function of time during the first three hours of their hike.

 C. The decrease in the elevation per hour of the group during the first three hours of hiking.

 D. The increase in the elevation per hour of the group during the first three hours of hiking.

**Answer:** D

**Explanation:** The equation h=736t+3210 modeling the elevation as a function of time has the form of the equation of the line in slope-intercept form y=mx+b. The variable m is the slope, and the variable b is the initial elevation. The variable m is equal to 736. The variable t is time in hours. The equation describes the elevation in feet. Therefore, the 736 is the increase in elevation per hour during the first three hours of the group's hike. It is an increase because the slope is positive.

## QUESTION 55

If $a^{\frac{1}{3}}=y$, where a>0 and y>0, which of the following equations gives a in terms of y?

   A. $a=-y^3$

   B. $a=\dfrac{1}{y^3}$

   C. $a=-\dfrac{1}{y^3}$

   D. $a=y^3$

**Answer:** B

**Explanation:** Solve the equation for a by using the rules of exponents.

$$a^{\frac{1}{3}}=y$$

Raise both sides to an exponent of -3.

$$\left(a^{\frac{1}{3}}\right)^{-3}=(y)^{-3}$$

$$a=y^{-3}$$

$$a=\frac{1}{y^3}$$

# PRAXIS® 5169 Middle School Mathematics

## The PRAXIS® Series

CPSIA information can be obtained
at www.ICGtesting.com
Printed in the USA
LVOW04s1335260617

539409LV00010B/112/P

9 781537 570747